Navigating the River of Grief

A Guide for Pastors and Counselors

BONNIE BATES

FIRST EDITION
Copyright © 2017
by CSS Publishing Co., Inc.

Library of Congress Cataloging-in-Publication Data

Names: Bates, Bonnie, author.
Title: Navigating the river of grief / by Bonnie Bates.
Description: FIRST EDITION. | Lima : CSS Publishing Company, Inc., 2018.
Identifiers: LCCN 2017049773 | ISBN 9780788028854 (pbk. : alk. paper)
Subjects: LCSH: Church work with the bereaved. | Grief--Religious aspects--Christianity. | Pastoral theology.
Classification: LCC BV4330 .B38 2018 | DDC 259/.6--dc23
LC record available at https://lccn.loc.gov/2017049773

e-book:
ISBN-13: 978-0-7880-2886-1
ISBN-10: 0-7880-2886-3

ISBN-13: 978-0-7880-2885-4
ISBN-10: 0-7880-2885-5

Contents

Acknowledgments

I would be remiss if I didn't thank those who have made this work possible. I want to thank especially the faculty of Colgate Rochester Crozer Divinity School for the opportunity to engage in doctoral work. I want to specifically thank Mark Brummit, who served as my doctoral dissertation mentor and advisor, for his wisdom, insight and challenge to dig deeper into the work. I want to thank Stephanie Sauve for her support and wisdom through both my M.Div. and D.Min. experiences. I want to thank Robert Spilman who served as an additional reader and helped me encounter and respond to my own river of grief through his leadership in my Clinical Pastoral Education experience.

I also want to thank those who were willing to discuss their river of grief experiences with me as a part of my research for this work. Their vulnerability, sharing and trust are to be admired and this work could not have been completed without them.

I could not have completed my studies or this work without the ongoing support and love of my husband, Steve Vulcheff. Without him I could have accomplished none of this. Steve continues to light up my life with joy, hope, and love.

Disclaimer

To protect the identities and personal experiences of those with whom I explored the topics and experiences of grief and mourning, I have changed their names, but not their stories.

Introduction

The aim of this book is to reflect on situations of lament, grief, crisis, trauma, and the role of pastoral support so that guidance can be provided by ministers as they accompany congregants on the grief journey. As a minster in the United Church of Christ, I have a myriad of experiences with loss and mourning. These moments are profoundly impactful on the individuals encountering the loss and the grief, as well as the friends, fellow church members, and pastors of the bereaved. As I worked with people, comforting those approaching death, sitting with families in hospital waiting rooms and hospice in-patient facilities, talked with families as we planned together the memorialization of the life of their loved one, and officiated at memorial, funeral, or celebration of life services, I came to be intrigued by the process of grief and the navigation of the grief process.

From these experiences I began to wonder how other people might have been comforted, challenged, assisted, or hindered during their grief process, or their sense of loss, by the words of pastors, hymns, scripture, and worship. There are few human universal truths and birth and death are among them. "To live a human life is to experience loss and grief."

As I reflected on grief, I found myself dissatisfied with the models I had read about or had been lectured about. Thus I developed a new model for the grief process, the *River of Grief* model. I came to view grief as a river to be navigated. There is the entry point, the loss, which pushes the individual into a river of emotions and challenges. As progress down this river occurs, the course is rocky or calm, sometimes alternately, but the journey continues. We might choose to avoid or deny the river of loss and grief, but in that case the river is encountered in other ways, which is similar to a flood of chaos and emotion at some other point in time, like a flooding river looking for the path of least resistance. Rivers begin to flow, cease to flow, seem to fold back on themselves, have shallows and rapids, and are unpredictable. This has been my own experience with grief and has been the experience of others with whom I have spoken. Grief is not a linear process, but was found to be a circuitous journey which requires courage, confidence, support, and assistance to navigate. My exploration of grief as a process and a river to navigate led me to seek answers to some fundamental questions about grief, the grieving, and the journey grief takes us humans on.

Questions About The Journey

We ask questions about the grief journey. What helps us stay afloat as we journey through grief? How do others navigate the river of grief and loss? Who accompanies us on the river, guiding, steering, partnering on the journey? Do pastors know how to journey with their congregation members as they take this challenging journey? How do pastors calm their own fears, anxieties, or sense of loss? What boundaries do pastors need to set in order to be spiritually, emotionally, and physically healthy enough to support their congregations during the grief process? How do congregation members articulate what they need and receive, what they need and don't receive, what they receive and didn't know they needed, or what they didn't receive that they now know would have been helpful to them? Could pastors support the grief journey more effectively? Could worship and preaching impact the connection with God in spite of, or because of, the lament, grief, crisis, or trauma? All these questions need answers and the aim here is to reflect on situations of lament, grief, crisis, trauma and the role of pastoral support so both the mourner and the pastor can navigate the grief journey more effectively.

Accompanying The River Travelers

As individuals encounter experiences of grief, the roles pastors play and messages pastors provide impact, either positively or negatively, how faith was, and is, viewed, deepened, and appreciated by the individual. The pastoral response could move an individual or a family closer to God and relationship with God or further away from God and relationship with God. Similarly the pastoral response could also move the individual or family toward the faith community or away from the faith community.

Enlightening the pastor and, in some ways, the congregation becomes vital to the retention of relationships with God and the faith community in times of grief.

Individuals come to pastors seeking understanding, solace, empathy, counsel, and a range of other supports while they are grieving. Individuals need more than the preparation of the memorial or funeral service. They need more than clichés about God's presence or God's will. What helps individuals varies by gender, age, race, class, and religious experience. Yet, each individual needs assistance, nurturing, and support from various sources. How a pastor helps an individual navigate the River of Grief and grounds the grief experience is important. The pastor impacts the way individuals began to or continue to see God as present with them.

It is possible for a pastor to focus on the mechanics of navigating the River of Grief and to fail to mention or engage the spiritual aspects of the grief journey. Various authors talk about the tasks of grief and the work of grief. Not so many authors write about the spiritual aspects of grief and the development of a new or different relationship with God through the navigation of grief. Pastors are a part of the journey individuals take as they seek to complete the tasks and accomplish the work of grief. Pastors also have an essential role in the spiritual part of the River of Grief.

Methodology For This Manuscript's Development

As a Doctor of Ministry student at the Colgate Rochester Crozer Divinity School in Rochester, New York, I undertook this project as a doctoral dissertation. Throughout the process I researched a variety of grief models and theories: Kubler Ross, Lindemann, Bowlby, Sullender, Syreeni, Murray Parkes, Marris, Davidson, Devaul, and Zisook.

While conducting research on the formation of theories about and models of grief, I also prepared to have qualitative, reflection interviews with those who had experienced grief within the last two years. The model I used for conducting the qualitative interviews was based on David McMahill's work *"Completing the Circle: Reviewing Ministries in Congregations."*[1]

As the reflection interviews were concluded, I explore the theological underpinnings of attitudes about grief and our relationship with God. Psalm 30 became the basis for this theological exploration. I particularly found

1   McMahill, David. "Completing the Circle: Reviewing Ministries in Congregations" (Lanham. MD: Rowman & Littlefield Publishers, 2003).

direction in verse 5b, "Weeping may linger for the night, but joy comes with the morning"(NRSV). This verse spoke to me of the change process human beings experience as time passes. A journey through the night into the morning is expressed in the psalm. A journey from the darkness of sorrow and into the light of hope is expressed in the journey of grief.

While this book results from a doctoral dissertation, it is my hope that ministers, both ordained and lay, and those exploring providing support for all those who are grieving will find the text informative and generative, birthing new ideas and plans for relational support for brothers and sisters encountering all forms of grief. The Navigating The River Of Grief model may be helpful. Hearing the needs and desires of the grieving who were interviewed may be helpful. Exploring our individual grief narratives may be helpful. I would like to know what you find helpful in this text, what challenges you, and what you flat out disagree about. Engage the text and engage me in your exploration. May God bless us as we navigate all the journeys of our lives.

Note: The names used in this book are fictional and do not relate to any particular person.

Chapter 1
Models Of Grief

A variety of stages of grief have been developed, but it is important for the clergy person to remember each individual encounters grief differently and works through the grief tasks at difference pace. Westberg mentioned ten stages of grief; Kubler-Ross identified five stages of grief. There is a newer model, "the Bowlby-Parkes Attachment model which defined four phases (numbing — yearning and searching — disorganization (sic)/depression — reorganization (sic)/recovery)."[2]

From my perspective and in my experience, the number of stages was less important than understanding that the grief process may always be changing and evolving for the individual. Most of these theorists focused on a linear and chronological progression of the grief process. Their research was about identifying stages or steps and the interventions which helped people move from one stage or step to the next. While some progression through stages was identified in my research, the process and progression by the bereaved with whom I spoke was neither linear nor chronological.

R. Scott Sullender indicated the need to understand the grief process as a changing and evolving process in his research of grief models. He also asserted that the nature and extent of a person's grief is varied and changes based on the situation, that grief reactions vary widely, and that there was a cultural component to grief. He explored three models:

2   Bowlby, John. *Attachment and Loss Volume 3* (3 volumes: Hammondsworth: Penguin, 1969-1980). pp. 85-96.

1. Grief as reaction to loss — any life change can be a loss event and therefore potentially an occasion for grief.
2. Grief as separation anxiety — acute grief can be similar to an anxiety attack and thus talking as a way symbolically and conceptually staying close to the lost love object is still the best remedy.
3. Grief as a function of attachment instincts — grief exists because the griever valued and gave meaning to that which is now lost.[3]

Sullender noted interdependence in the three models but indicated that each has a different and unique perspective into the nature of grief and mourning. Still Sullender did not enlighten us to the repetitive nature of grief, the folding back on itself and the repetition of steps or stages within the grief process. The approach was to understand grief, but to do so in an intellectual and linear manner, rather than a holistic and spiritual approach.

Syreeni focused on the Bowlby Model, speaking of the transitions between the stages of grief as the more important focus. He described the initial reaction as one of feeling that the deceased person was still present or may return soon. The bereaved might see the deceased in dreams or visions, hear the voice of the deceased, or even search for them in familiar places. The middle stage was the acceptance of the loss, the knowledge that the deceased would not be returning. This was when emotional responses such as anger, self-reproach or regret, depression, or despair might be experienced. The end stage as defined by Syreeni was reached when the individual has accepted their changed existence, their new life, without

3   Sullender, R. Scott, "Three Theoretical Approaches to Grief," The Journal of Pastoral Care (December 1979), pp 243-51 as quoted in Sunderland, Ronald H. Getting Through Grief: Caregiving by Congregations. (Nashville: Abingdon Press, 1993), pp 31-32.

the deceased. At this end stage some of the individuals' coping mechanisms kicked in and acceptance began to take place.[4] While the transitions were important, Syrenni once again focused on the need to move the bereaved through a linear process, without any consideration of the regression, as well as progression, which is a part of the grief process for bereaved individuals.

DeVaul and Zisook developed a three stage model which incorporated "shock, acute mourning, and resolution. [5] Stone expanded this process and indicated seven stages of grief: "shock, catharsis, depression, guilt, preoccupation with loss, anger, and adaptation to reality."[6] Yet again, they focused on a linear progressive model with no mention of spirituality and no recognition of the regression or progression between stages.

As we move into the next section of this work, I use an adaptation of the Sunderland Model, a four step process, for the work of mourning.[7] The model designed by Sunderland seemed effective in an exploration of steps for navigating the River of Grief. There were a couple of differences in my approach to grief, and a specific reason why the River of Grief model has such meaning for

4   Syreeni, Kari. "In Memory of Jesus: Grief Work in the Gospels," *Biblical Interpretation* Volume 12, Number 2, pp 2-3

5   DeVaul, R and Zisook, S. "Unresolved Grief Clinical Considerations," *Postgraduate Medicine*, 1961, Volume 59, pp 267-271, as quoted in Ingram, Hurley, & Riley, "Grief-Resolution Therapy in a Pastoral Context," *The Journal of Pastoral Care*, Volume 39, Number 1, 1985, p 70.

6   Stone, HW. *Suicide and Grief* (Philadelphia: Fortress Press, 1972) as quoted in Ingram, Hurley, & Riley, "Grief-Resolution Therapy in a Pastoral Context," *The Journal of Pastoral Care*, Volume 39, Number 1, 1985, p 70.

7   Sunderland, Ronald H. Getting Through Grief: Caregiving by Congregations. (Nashville: Abingdon Press, 1993), pp 37-39.

me. Firstly, the spiritual component of grief was, and is, of deep importance to me. As a pastor who has been actively engaged in pastoral care, I have seen the impact of faith, lack of faith, experiencing a community of faith and the catharsis of lament and the peace-giving of hope in my work with the bereaved. Secondly, in my pastoral experience, and through the interviews I conducted, which will be discussed later in this work, I have seen the flow of the River of Grief. I have seen individuals move through the entry phase of the River of Grief, move into navigating the River and then come back to their entry point, with the emotional anger, denial, and bargaining of which Kübler-Ross has written. I adapted the Sunderland model reflecting the pastoral support necessary, the spiritual components of the grief process and scriptural resources found to be helpful as each step of the grief journey is navigated.

The work of mourning

As mentioned above, it is the work of mourning on which caregivers need to focus and where pastors can provide guidance and influence. The work of mourning has four major steps with subsets of stages to move through. The steps are: accepting the reality of the loss, working through the painful feelings, struggling back through depression, and deciding to take up one's life again. As the steps of the journey were explored, pastoral care implications, spiritual development implications, and scriptural supports are shared. Additionally, anecdotal information shared by grief travelers was included, reflecting their step on the journey and their encounters with God as each step was encountered.

Step One - Accepting the reality of the loss

The first of the major steps is accepting the reality of the loss. This involved a focus on the real loss of the person and the understanding that the person was no longer physically available. Within this step tasks included: emancipation from bondage to the deceased — the acceptance that the person is gone and will not return; accepting the pain and readjusting to the environment — the acceptance of the emotional and physical pain of loss and making the adjustment to a world without that person in it. This step can take a short or a long time, regardless of the connection or depth of relationship. The transition through this step had more to do with the individual and their ability to manage feelings than it had to the particularity of the relationship.[8]

Numbness was found to be a valid initial response to loss. No matter how prepared individuals felt they were, shock and numbness were likely to be the first feelings encountered by the bereaved. In the case of unexpected loss, intense feelings of shock and numbness were common. All losses found individuals unprepared. There was an anesthetic effect to the shock and numbness which helped the bereaved move through the first moments or days of the grief journey. A prolonged period of numbness sometimes resulted in denial of the loss or of the feelings of loss. This required different interventions with the bereaved.

At this point in the River of Grief journey, pastoral presence was vitally important. Support offered prior to the loss, at the very moment of the loss, and/or immediately after the loss had benefits for the bereaved. Support prior to a loss usually involved an individual who

8   Ibid.

was terminally ill and their family and caregivers. Unless the pastor had a relationship with the individual and the family, it was unlikely the pastor would have an opportunity to provide support prior to the actual loss. If the terminally ill individual or the family was known to the pastor, preparation for the loss included equipping the family and caregivers with prayer support through individual, group or congregational prayers, offering scripture and hymns as a means of preparing for the transition, an anointing of the individual who was ill, exploring anticipatory grief issues through discussion, or involved a ministry of presence, simply being with the terminally ill individual and their family and caregivers. Discussions led by the pastor included the asking of questions such as:

- How are you encountering God in this time?
- What hopes or fears do you have surrounding the end of your life?
- How can I ease your pain or assist you?
- What provisions or plans have you made for the end of your life? Do you want to be at home, in a hospital, in a hospice center?
- Where do you need my presence during this process?

Asking questions enabled the individual and the family to have some control over the support and the resources a pastor shared with them. At a time when many things, including physical condition, were beyond the control of the individual, choices became even more important. With regards to anticipatory grief, it was important for the family to understand the concept and to be aware that the dying individual was likely to compress his/her circle of contact, eliminating contact with the outside world, with friends and distant family, as they prepared to say goodbye to their earthly existence.

Support at the moment of loss usually involved being present with the family, individual and/or caregivers when the end of life was near. Once again prayer support, scripture reading, the singing of hymns, and the ministry of presence were important pastoral supports. In the reflection interview information, Tabitha, Sandy, Liza, and Candy all mentioned the ministry of presence as a pastoral support and its importance to them. Whether the dying individual was in the hospital, in a hospice facility or at home, the pastor's presence with the family was a comfort to all involved in the process. Even if the dying individual was unconscious, prayers, anointing, touching, and speaking with the individual made a difference. In one encounter I had with a congregant who was in a coma in the hospital, my touch during anointing and prayer initiated a soft hum from Tom indicating his knowledge of the touch. In my experiences with neurologists and other physicians, I have been told that touch and hearing are the last senses to diminish when an individual is in a coma or near death. Touching, praying, and talking were important parts of the support at the moments just before and at the moment of loss. These three actions engage the body, the mind, and the spirit.

At this point of the grief process, the bereaved were just entering the journey. They needed time alone with the deceased, time to weep and keen, time to kiss and hug their loved one. The pastor's role shifted to one of presence, patiently accompanying the bereaved in this initial stage of loss. There came a time when offering a prayer, singing a hymn, or embracing the bereaved was important, but the simple ministry of presence was needed as the bereaved prepared to enter the river of grief which would consume their days and nights in the weeks to come.

Recently I had the honor of being present with a man at the moment of his wife's death. I read scriptures, a psalm he felt was particularly meaningful to him. We prayed together for her safe passage from this world into the next. I blessed her and anointed her. As I concluded the blessing, she slipped peacefully from this world. The holiness of the moment was so clear to all of us gathered there. The prayers and anointing were important, but for this gentleman my presence was the most valuable of the gifts he identified. Tabitha and Liza specifically mentioned the sharing of prayers as a means of pastoral support. Candy mentioned listening as an important pastoral support. For Liza, Bob, and Christine the singing of hymns in the hospital room was a source of pastoral support.

As the bereaved began to navigate the River of Grief, there were additional pastoral supports needed and required. It was important for the pastor to understand that while progress through this first step could be clearly identified; regression back to this first step was possible, a renewed denial that the death had occurred or that the loved one was never coming back, could easily overtake one's journey through the River of Grief.

Step Two – Working through painful feelings

The second major step was working through painful feelings, feelings that could burden and overwhelm. The feelings included feelings of shock, numbness, and disbelief encountered during mourning. Anger, depression, loneliness, isolation, alienation, helplessness, panic, shame, guilt, remorse, guilt, fear, anxiety, despair, relief, or emancipation might be felt by an individual. These were appropriate feelings and individuals needed to be counseled to feel what they were feeling and to acknowledge the confusion or feelings that might be persisting. Anger was often the first emotion — either anger at the individual who had died or at the perceived causes of the loss.

Managing Anger

The first task of working through painful feelings was to manage the anger. Safety to express the anger was necessary for the anger's resolution or management. The need to express the anger was important and space must be given for the anger to be expressed in order for the feeling to be managed. It was important to note that anger may make the task of mourning more painful or prolonged. Instances of tragedy, either real or perceived, often resulted in anger.

Often anger or frustration was a form of grieving, but sometimes the anger and frustration were truly anger. It seemed natural to feel furious about loss especially in the case of accidental death, sudden death, or the death of an infant or child. Anger could be aimed at the self for not preventing the accident or death, at a family member who had recently died, at the physicians and caregivers who provided medical care to the deceased or at God for letting the death occur at all. Lois mentioned her anger at the medical professionals who failed to treat a diagnosed injury, the ignoring of which may have precipitated her husband's death. Bob mentioned his own self-anger and recrimination because he was driving the car in which Sophie was injured.

Deep seated anger needs to be expressed before the bereaved can continue the grief journey. In our western culture, anger is sometimes a more acceptable emotion than grief, especially in men. Therefore, men will mask their sorrow with anger. Pastors need to assist the bereaved to express and understand their anger by asking questions, such as those suggested in *Good Mourning*, a text by Allan Hugh Cole, Jr.:

- "Is the anger an expression of sadness that you find difficult to express?
- If so, then what lies behind your responding in an angry manner?
- Some of us accept and tolerate anger, frustration, or impatience more readily than we do feeling sad or despairing. Does this describe you and your experience?"[9]

Pastors need to help the bereaved move past the attitude that anger is a sin or that its expression is sinful. God's anger is expressed in scripture. Jesus' anger is expressed in scripture. The concept that anger itself is not sinful needed to be shared. The behaviors resulting from anger might be sinful. This understanding of anger can relieve some of the guilt associated with anger and has helped the mourning individual to move through anger and from anger to acceptance more readily.[10]

While a more in-depth exploration of scripture is provided in the next chapter, I mention a few examples here. Pastors can cite or share these scriptural passages as they may be important to the bereaved's acceptance of their feelings of anger. While Hebrew scripture passages about the wrath of God often have connotations of God's anger at sin, human death saddens God and can result in God's anger. Approaching the Christian scriptures allowed us to reflect on God's love as the theme, but

9   Cole, Allan Hugh Jr., *Good Mourning: Getting Through Your Grief.* (Lousiville: Westminster John Knox Press, 2008). p 12

10   Sunderland, pp 40-42

God's anger at human disobedience and transgression is still a part of this section of the canon. Scripture passages reflecting God's or Jesus' anger include: Exodus 4:14, Deuteronomy 29:23, 2 Samuel 6:7, Psalm 103:8, Joel 2:13, and John 2:13-17. Paul's theology also includes wrath and he mentions it in relation to "human disobedience and transgression"[11] and God's anger as a result: Romans 1:18;2:5; 2:8; 5:9; 9:22; Ephesians 2:3; 5:6; Colossians 3:6; and 1 Thessalonians 1:10.[12] Biblical references to anger shared by pastors or ministers, can allow the bereaved to share their own feelings of anger.

Aside from anger, the bereaved also experienced feelings of regret which needed to be worked through and laid aside. This task is explored next.

Laying Aside Regret

The second task of working through painful feelings was to lay aside regrets. Regrets stem from real or imagined omissions, and if regret was not addressed it often resulted in lifelong remorse. Candy recalled her regret at not being present with her mother at the time of her death, and having not spoken to her on the phone the previous day. In spite of Candy's years of care, her mother's death occurring during Candy's vacation was a source of regret. Self-blame is at the root of regret and may be caused by being involved in a tragedy, as when a parent is driving the car in which an accident results in the death of a child. Regret moved the bereaved into bargaining, and was filled with the "if only" expression. Individuals felt that something could have been done by

11   *Harper Collins Bible Dictionary.* Achtemeier, Paul J.editor. (New York: HarperSanFrancisco, 1996), p 1227.

12   Ibid. pp 1226-1227.

them to prevent the death. Confronting regret and guilt were an important part of managing the tasks of grief.[13]

Regret came from realizing that life would not be the same without the loved one. Since they were gone they can no longer experience life with them or enjoy the relationship. They regret the loss of the relationship. There were more specific reasons cited for feelings of regret. These included "the inability to have said 'goodbye' to the deceased, dissatisfaction over some aspect of the relationship we had with the deceased, feelings of neglect of the deceased or the relationship with the deceased, or perhaps feelings of shame over who we have been or failed to be in relation to the deceased."[14] The danger of regret was that it could grow into guilt and guilt crippled the River of Grief journeyer and prevented them from progressing along the river.

Often pastors find themselves in positions of hearing the confessions of regrets of the bereaved. Listening became the primary pastoral support in this instance. No pastor was able to remove the regrets that a bereaved individual felt. Pastors could only accompany the bereaved along this stage of working through painful feelings. Forgiveness is a theological concept that was important in the laying aside of regret. While it will be discussed later in this work, conversations surrounding the theology of salvation and forgiveness needed to be explored at this step of the journey. Pastors were able to help the bereaved in building an understanding of the concept of forgiveness. Clinging to God's forgiveness in the storm of regret was one of the only ways through this stage. Scriptural references that shared the steadfast love of God and God's forgiveness were important to share at this stage of

13   Sunderland, pp 42-43

14   Cole, p 15

the River of Grief journey. Scripture passages used at this stage of the journey could be: Psalm 32, Matthew 6:14-15, Luke 6:37, Luke 7:47-50, Romans 4:7-8, Ephesians 4:31-32, Colossians 2:6-14, James 5:13-15, and 1 John 2:12-14.

As this step in the journey was completed, the struggle with sadness is likely to continue. This task of working through painful feelings is now explored.

Struggling through Sadness

The third task of working through the painful feelings was struggling through the sadness. Symptoms of bereavement were often similar to the symptoms of depression — feelings of emotional distance, tightness in the throat, weakness, tension or mental pain, and sighing may be physical symptoms of bereavement. Deep and clinical depression needed psychological counseling or even medical intervention. In most cases was, the need was to clarify the sadness in relation to the loss. In this instance the intervention of a pastor was essential.

The bereaved may have been encouraged to "be strong" which sometimes was interpreted as not feeling or expressing sadness. Sadness needed to be expressed, as the failure to do so could have resulted in crippling despair. The longer the period of crippling despair and hopelessness, the more likely the feelings were to become destructive.[15] We, especially in the west, have some level of discomfort with expressions of sadness. Pastoral counselors needed to set aside their personal discomfort with expressions of sadness and allow the expression to flow freely from the bereaved individual. The keening and wailing in days past were important emotional releases for the bereaved. As pastors and spiritual co-journeyers, we needed uncover our own discomfort with sadness

15   Ibid, p 12

and assist the bereaved in feeling what they felt at this step in the River of Grief journey. Avoidance of the sadness added an unnecessary burden to the bereaved and indicated a lack of concern for the loss. Protecting the individual from feeling the sadness and expressing it was a mistake and hindered the work of struggling with and through the sadness.[16]

We often intellectualize death, using our rational mind as a shield to the deep emotions and sadness that need expressing. Jerome Miller stated,

"The therapeutic effort to bring grief into the open, to talk about death without our old hesitancies and reluctances, is often motivated by a desire so to transform the experience of death that we can undergo it without being ultimately upset by it. But the sufferer may be close to discovering a truth that the therapeutic way of thinking never leads us to suspect — that our whole ordinary way of life, with all its evasions and avoidances, is in some profound sense unreal. Suffering has a way of turning everything upside down. And from that overturned perspective, it makes no sense to resume one's ordinary life — because one knows now the truths it was designed to keep hidden."[17]

Rather than focusing on the therapeutic and intellectual, or even the psychological approach to the emotions associated with grief, it was more advantageous for pastors to utilize a spiritual approach. Recognizing the human emotions, finding these emotions expressed in scripture or hymnody or even contemporary music had a profound effect in moving from the denial of feelings to their expression.

16 Sunderland, pp 43-46

17 Vaughn, F. Bruce. "Recovering Grief in the Age of Grief Recovery," *The Journal of Pastoral Theology*. Vol. 13. No. 1, June 2003, p. 37

Pastoral support during the bereaved's process of working through this third painful feeling included the planning for, preparation of, and conducting of a funeral, memorial service and/or graveside service. The time spent with the family remembering the bereaved was very beneficial in allowing the sadness and despair to be shared and expressed. During our interview, Micah recalled the importance of being able to tell the story of the life of the deceased and the relationships and history shared by the deceased and the bereaved. It was as if the pastor helped with the tasks involved in managing the sadness by giving opportunity for expression and remembering.

Denominational resources for funeral planning are readily available, but literature, poetry, and more contemporary worship resources were also helpful. Discussions with the family included whether or not calling hours at a funeral home or a wake would be a part of the preparation for the funeral or memorial service. Family customs and expectations need to be considered, as does the health and coping ability of the bereaved. Family members needed to be assured, by the pastor, that they had choices in the worship services and the celebration of the deceased's life.

Pastors needed to probe with the family their concepts of heaven, salvation and the afterlife. While a theological discussion was warranted, simplifying the denomination doctrine of salvation was necessary here. This was not a lecture or a bible study, but a time to ensure the funeral service reflected both the denomination and the beliefs of the family. Questions included:

- Where do you think your loved one is right now?
- How do you view heaven? How is the deceased greeted in heaven?

- How do you see the presence of God present with your relative now?
- How are you feeling the presence of God now?
- What words of comfort about heaven and salvation do you need to hear at the funeral, memorial or graveside service?
- Do you want prayers only with the family at the funeral home or prayers with all those gathered?
- Should military honors or fraternal order honors be planned for?

Once again, scriptural references were comforting at this point in the grief journey. Some psalms were especially comforting, as were portions of the gospels. Although a more in depth discussion of scriptures is found in the next chapter of this text, suggested resources were: Psalm 103, John 10, John 14, Romans 8, 1 Corinthians 15, and Colossians 3. Psalms of Lament that are outlined in chapter four of this work are helpful to both the pastor co-journeyer and the bereaved journeyer.

As the acknowledgment of sadness was navigated and the memorial service was concluded, the pastor needed to help the bereaved prepare for struggling back from depression. This is explored in the next section of the text.

Step Three – Struggling back from depression

The third major step of working through grief was struggling back from depression. Depression is sometimes clinical in nature and this condition requires medication to correct shifts and changes in the human body. But often the depression discussed in relation to bereavement was situational depression, the continuing sorrow based on an occurrence or action. The depths of depression can cause the bereaved to stop working through the grief process, and to cease moving forward through the current of time. "Bereaved people learn to 'let the past go' and turn their minds toward the future.[18] This involved facing the future, however bleak or dark or burdened the future might seem. Symptoms of depression could be mild or severe during the grief period. An inability to personally work through the depression sometimes required psychological or medical intervention. The depression in these cases had a biological component, a chemical imbalance caused by a preexisting tendency toward depression or a chemical imbalance which was stress induced. However, in many cases the milder symptoms involved the bereaved using their own strength and hope to move from the depressive state.

The support and encouragement from the pastor, the family, and other support groups were essential to this task. The stronger the individual felt, the stronger their self-esteem, the stronger their personal sense of hope was, the more likely the bereaved individual was to be able to struggle to leave behind the depression. When the bereaved felt that their depression was "normal" they were more likely to be successful in struggling through it.

In my own pastoral experience, I have encountered individuals whose family and friends think the bereaved needed to "get over it" and move on with their life. To a depressed individual, there was no concept of "getting over it." For some individuals, the depression encountered seemed insurmountable. One individual likened it to being in a long dark tunnel, feeling closed in, with no sign of light or no vision of the end of the tunnel. There was no way to "get over it." Remarks such has these impeded rather than assisted the individuals to move

18   Ibid. p 46

through depression. Reminding individuals that their grief experience is what it is, that grief is managed and moved through differently by each bereaved person, was very important. Being sad, being depressed and feeling trapped in the sadness were real parts of the grief journey. If cases where the pastor or family saw the bereaved individual as not able to normalize their depression or saw the symptoms linger or worsen, medical or psychological intervention was necessary.[19] The pastor needed to pay attention to and spend some time with the bereaved in order to make this assessment.

Pastoral roles included the ministry of listening; visiting with the bereaved and allowing them time to share what they are feeling at this point of the journey. This was the point in the journey where a grief support program offered by the church or the community could be suggested to the bereaved. Both formal and informal grief support groups were helpful to the bereaved. The sharing of the loss with those on a similar journey was very helpful to the bereaved. It was good for them to understand others' feelings and to identify with others who have experienced similar grief. Bob mentioned receiving some resources from his pastor which helped him understand the depth of what he was feeling throughout his River of Grief journey. The specific resources are discussed later in this chapter, but written materials can be helpful to the bereaved.

If the bereaved has not returned to church attendance or other social activities, encouragement needs to be provided to him or her. This is further discussed in the next section of the text as the flow of the River of Grief continues.

19   Ibid. pp. 46-47

Step Four – Deciding to take up one's life again

The fourth major step in working through grief was to decide to take up one's life again, a different life certainly, but a life with a past, a present and a future. This involved the bereaved individual returning to daily routine tasks, regular activities and responsibilities. When a death or loss intervenes in an individual's life, it was necessary and expected that routine tasks would not be the focus. Working through anger, depression, and regret impacted an individual's ability to manage routine tasks. Individuals were cognizant of this and for a while accepted this inability.

Returning to regular daily life was one of the most difficult tasks for the bereaved. Returning to one's regular life seemed like a betrayal, a moving away from the care and loss, a denial of the strength of the relationship or the importance of the deceased. However, pastors need to be able to help individuals recognize the importance of regaining footing in routine and daily tasks, work, hobbies, housekeeping, sports, and groups. All these provided a sense of normalcy to the bereaved individual and helped them transition out of anger, regret and depression. The memory of the deceased became the focus in the life of the bereaved. Some of the anger had dissipated. Some of the regret had diminished. Some of the physical and emotional pain had been deadened. Depressive symptoms had abated. This was the stage where the bereaved began to reclaim her or his life, the life that would continue without the loved one.[20] Lois, Candy, Liza, and Christine all mentioned the need to get on with routine chores and regular work routines as being helpful to them. Work and household chores provided a distraction, something

20   Ibid. pp. 47-49

else for them to focus on and gave them a way to move beyond their grief.

Pastoral and spiritual support continued to be important at this stage of the journey. Once again a ministry of presence was important. A card sent or phone call to the bereaved was appreciated. A visit to check on how the grief journey is progressing was vital. The pastor who had a good relationship with the bereaved noticed if lingering signs of depression were present, if additional emotional supports were needed, and could help determine if the bereaved had reengaged with their new life. Particular questions were useful at this point of the journey:

How are you doing?
Where are you feeling the presence of God in your days? Your nights?
What changes have you made to your daily routine?
What social activities are you getting to?
How is the rest of your family doing?
What are you hoping for these days?
What is still really uncomfortable for you to think about or do?

As these questions were answered and discussed, the pastor needed to offer additional prayer or scriptural resources, suggestions for engaging with the church community, or perhaps the establishment of an individual to accompany the bereaved as he or she continues the journey with may be in order. If there were Stephen Ministers[21] or a Called to Care[22] group established in the

21 Stephen Ministry, accessed at http://www.stephenministries.org/stephenministry/default.cfm/917 on September 25, 2010.

22 Called to Care, accessed at http://www.calledtocare.com on September 25, 2010.

church, some communication with them about ongoing support to the bereaved was planned. Individuals are unique and the level of accompaniment they seek was as varied as the individuals, but a plan for ongoing support needed to be developed to assure the bereaved was not feeling abandoned.

Chapter 2
An Overview Of The River Of Grief Model

The Sunderland Model provided a background for understanding the River of Grief. The stages that Sunderland identified are: shock, denial, anger, guilt, sorrow and depression, acceptance, and engaging life.[23] The River of Grief Model provides an opportunity to understand grief and the stages and steps of grief by looking at a natural phenomenon.

Water is used scripturally as a sign of cleansing, as in baptism; as a sign of chaos, as in the uncontrolled waters before God's ordering of creation; as a passageway from danger into safety, like the passing through the Red Sea or across the Jordan River into the promised land. In this chapter, I clarify how I used the River of Grief model by linking it with the Sunderland steps of managing grief.[24]

Stage One – Entering the River of Grief

The first major stage of the River of Grief is entering. This stage aligns with Sunderland's step of accepting the reality of the loss. As a fly-fishing angler, I understand the challenge of entering a river. One needs to consider the depth of the river, the current, one's safety and one's equipment and clothing. There are decisions to be made about where to enter the river, how to enter the river, and the safety considerations of entering the river alone or being accompanied.

23 http://www.journey-through-grief.com/7-stages-of-grief.html accessed on December 16, 2014

24 Sunderland, Ronald H. Getting Through Grief: Caregiving by Congregations. (Nashville: Abingdon Press, 1993)

For the bereaved, there was little choice about whether or not to enter the river. A loss occurred and the bereaved entered the River of Grief. They may have done so unwillingly, burying feelings of grief and loss, but they were grieving nonetheless. In some cases, entering the River of Grief included emancipation from the bondage of caring for the newly deceased. In all cases, entering the River of Grief required the acceptance that the deceased was gone and that pain and loss occurred. Given the ability, we would enter the River of Grief when we choose, but that option was rarely available to the bereaved. Rather, the bereaved enter the River of Grief as demanded by the loss and sought the equipment and accompaniment that made the entry safer and less isolating. Clothed with acceptance of the loss and recognizing the journey of grief as challenged by emotional and sometimes, physical pain, the bereaved entered the River of Grief.

Entering the River of Grief

Six of the bereaved I interviewed experienced anticipatory grief — three because of the illnesses of the deceased and three because of the injuries the deceased sustained prior to death. In no case did the anticipatory grief mitigate the total grief experiences or seem to shorten the River of Grief journey. Each individual entered the River of Grief at the point of loss, even if they had viewed the River of Grief, sat beside the river, and anticipated entering the river. The moments of anticipatory grief allowed the individuals to explore supports for the dying family member, a chance to explore the liturgical and ceremonial wishes of the dying, and time to share love and regret, but entering the River of Grief began at the moment of death.

In each case shock, emotional, physical and spiritual pain, anger, and profound feelings of loss were expressed. In cases where care-giving for the deceased had been a part of the role the bereaved filled, there was also some relief, and guilt at the feelings of relief. Even in cases of anticipatory grief, the moment of loss was deeply felt and had a profound impact on the bereaved. Those interviewed expressed some feelings of numbness and the inability to fathom what life would be like without their beloved family member.

Spiritually, the response was mixed. Some felt the comforting presence of God at the moment of loss, but for many there was a loss of that connection at the moment of the death of their loved one. Even in cases where the individual's faith was deep and mature, God's presence was not felt at the moment of the loss — often God's presence was felt before the loss and after the shock had abated, but at the moment of loss the spirits of those with whom I spoke seemed frozen, unable to be tapped into. This numbness was alluded to earlier in the previous chapter. For each of those I interviewed, the ministry of presence before and during the loss was cited as a gift from God. The presence of the pastor and one or two close friends was seen as the best support. Even when words were not spoken, even when prayers were not voiced, the simple ministry of presence at the point of the loss was a link to the bereaved's spiritual belief and sense of well-being.

Soon after the bereaved had entered the River of Grief, they begin their navigation process. We explore that part of the journey next.

Stage Two – Beginning to Navigate the River of Grief

The second major stage of the River of Grief is beginning to navigate. Navigation involved an understanding of the topography of the river banks, the flow and current of the river, the direction of that flow, and an understanding of the destination. Important at this stage of the River of Grief journey was understanding that grief is complex, involved, and requires time and energy to move through. At this stage, rivers of feelings seemed overwhelming. These feelings included shock, numbness, disbelief, anger, depression, loneliness, isolation, alienation, helplessness, panic, shame, guilt, remorse, fear, anxiety, despair, relief and/or emancipation. These feelings correlate with the first five steps of the Sunderland model.[25] As the bereaved began to navigate the River of Grief, an understanding of the whole river became helpful.

An awareness of the stages and process of grieving helps the bereaved move into this stage of the process. The River of Grief the bereaved is navigating is not some abstraction, but a real experience, with real rapids and shoals to be encountered. An equipping pastor might be able to shed some insight into the grief journey, by listening carefully to the bereaved and clarifying the "normalcy" of the grief. It is important for the bereaved to know the stages they might encounter, much as a cartographer might survey the river and its environs to assist future travelers.

Some bereaved linger at the beginning of the River of Grief navigation and encounter feelings of anger, shock, loneliness, alienation and the need to continue to express these and other emotions throughout the grieving process. Then they begin to be able to manage their emotions and move forward. Others seemed to stagnate, to

25   Ibid.

be stuck in the feelings of despair and depression. There are many challenges as the bereaved move into the next stage of navigating the River of Grief.

Beginning to Navigate the River of Grief

As time passed, in some cases only moments after the loss and in others a few days after the loss, the painful feelings became apparent and burdensome. The rivers of feelings included feelings of shock, numbness, and disbelief encountered during the mourning process. Those I interviewed felt anger, depression, loneliness, isolation, alienation, helplessness, panic, shame, guilt, remorse, guilt, fear, anxiety, despair, relief, or emancipation; some felt all these emotions, some only a few.

In one case, the bereaved had primary responsibility as the caregiver for her mother prior to death. Sandy began grieving for her mother as she was diagnosed with dementia and watched her personality and thought processes change. In this loss situation there was some relief that the burden of care was removed, although prior to the mother's death, Sandy's mother and her husband had moved into an assisted living facility which lightened the load, and allowed for some happiness to enter into the relationship. Sandy began navigating the River of Grief with a sense of relief that her mother was gone and was no longer suffering the illness that made relationships challenging for her and for the family. Entering the river seemed fairly easy for Sandy as she noted her loss began when her mother first started "disappearing" from her as a result of the dementia. Navigating the River of Grief allowed Sandy to reflect that her mother was freed from the confines of a mind that no longer allowed her to relate to her husband or her daughter. As Sandy began navigating the River of Grief, she expressed her belief that happiness would be possible for the mother in heaven; a happiness that had been lost during the last year of her illness. Sandy also shared her sense of the "keeping watch" period of time with me - the time when she watched as her mother approached death, and as she herself prepared to enter into and begin navigating the River of Grief. For Sandy there seemed less shock but a sense of inevitability that the River of Grief needed to be entered and navigated.

In the case of the death of Sophie, an accident was involved, so initially there was no sense of inevitability. That was yet to come. Sophie's husband was driving the car and apparently blacked out. He had no memory of the accident itself. He was one of my interviewees.

Sophie had been suffering from osteoarthritis and was becoming increasingly incapacitated. After the accident, the family was notified that the injuries were extensive and irreparable, exacerbated by her osteoarthritis, and that Sophie would likely die. At that moment, the inevitability of entering the River of Grief became apparent. They began to navigate the River of Grief before Sophie died. The family felt the shock of the accident — experiencing waves of emotion: anger, frustration, pain, sadness, irritability, and responsibility as they prepared to enter the River of Grief. There was also a sense of relief, for Sophie had made it clear that she didn't want to spend the end of her life in a nursing home, as her own mother had.

For this family, these bereaved, navigating the River of Grief came at the point of the loss, although they explored the river together with Sophie prior to the point of death. Each of her family members shared that Sophie was unafraid of the death to come. Her spirit and faith were strong. Sophie's strength of faith helped the family prepare to navigate the River of Grief. Bob, Sophie's husband, didn't want to talk about Sophie's impending death during her hospitalization. He felt responsible since he had been driving the car. He didn't know the extent of her injuries for a couple of days, as he was also injured in the accident. He expressed the loss that began before Sophie died. "It was hard to come home. I couldn't sleep. I changed beds but I would wake up calling her name," says Bob. They had been married nearly 61 years prior to the accident. The pain was still palpable in my conversation with Bob and the members of Sophie's family, tears welling their eyes as they re-experienced their entry into and their beginning navigation of the River of Grief. There was physical and spiritual pain as they recalled their anticipation of Sophie's death and their loss. Bob and the family had two weeks to accept the loss that was coming. That was their preparation period. The entry into and the navigating of the River of Grief began at the point of Sophie's death.

In each of the interviews, navigating the River of Grief was described as emotionally, spiritually and physically painful. Even in the case of Micah whose mother had lived in a supportive living environment for fifteen years, there was anger at the loss. Some of the anger was directed at a dependent sibling who had focused on her own needs and her own dependence rather than the needs of their mother. Micah, a serving pastor, felt the grief and anger even though he anticipated the loss of his mother, even though he had discussed life choices with her. Part of his grief and anger was based on the geographical distance between them and his inability to be physically present with her as often as he would have liked. Research indicated this part of the grief and anger is a natural occurrence, the pain of the loss of physical presence.[26] This is true of another of the bereaved I interviewed.

In several interviews, the "entering the river stage" of the River of Grief was complicated by relationships with other family members. In the case of Micah, the dependent relationship his sister had with their mother was a source of some of the anger at the impending loss. In the case of Sophie's daughter, the critical illness of the daughter Liza's son, was a source of anger and frustration.

Liza's son was in the hospital at the same time as Sophie suffering from pancreatitis brought on by his alcoholism. Liza shared the frustration of having to divide her time, the limited time she would have with Sophie whose injuries were not her "fault," and the time she felt she needed to spend with her son, whose illness she viewed as self-induced. Liza related, "I was conflicted part of the time while Mom was in the hospital as my son was in the hospital with pancreatitis and although the doctor didn't share it with me at the time, he was not expected to live. I couldn't figure out whom to be with first...I was conflicted because of my son — his pancreatitis was a result of his alcoholism and I felt sometimes like he was taking the attention away from Mom." This combination of the anger induced by entering the River of Grief and the anger at her son, never spilled into the relationship Liza had with her father Bob. Liza never expressed any anger at her father for the accident that led to Sophie's injuries.

Attention to the transition from life to death seemed important as family members prepared to navigate the River of Grief. Candy's mother died after a series of illnesses. She was away when her mother became ill and was hospitalized the last time. There was some guilt attached

26   Cole, Allan Hugh Jr., *Good Mourning: Getting Through Your Grief.* (Lousiville: Westminster John Knox Press, 2008).

to her absence at the time of death. Candy felt some relief after the loss, but also some guilt about that relief. There was the physical pain of the loss, the spiritual pain of the loss, but there was an element of physical relief, a release from the exhaustion Candy had been feeling as she cared for her mother. Yet, the loss of the physical presence of her mother still impacted Candy even nearly two years after the loss. Candy's mother was her cheerleader, the one who demonstrated unconditional love for her, who modeled empathy and compassion for Candy. Candy experienced the physical loss even today and the heaviness of the loss was evident in our conversation.

Entering and navigating the River of Grief was a profoundly challenging experience, physically, emotionally, spiritually, and intellectually. Even when the moment of death was anticipated, there was no real preparation for River of Grief entry or navigation. Even when the opportunity has been available for discussing the impending loss with the dying or with the family, the entry into and the beginning of the navigation of the River of Grief was a shock to the spirit, to the body, and to the mind of the bereaved.

Nowhere was this sense of shock to the spirit, body and mind clearer than in my conversation with Lois. Lois had entered the River of Grief three months before our conversation. Although her husband had some health problems, his death was the result of an injury after a fall, which was diagnosed but not treated. As such, Lois was still consumed by anger that medical professionals let a life-threatening injury go untreated. From her perspective, the loss of her husband was completely unnecessary.

Her grief was physically palpable in the tension of her shoulders, the wringing of her hands, and the tears freely flowing down her cheeks. She was navigating the River of Grief and her physical pain was very clear. Her mind was still trying to cope with the possibility that adequate treatment might have prevented her husband's death.

Additionally, Lois was coping with the intellectual strain of understanding all the scientific and medical evidence found after her husband's death, and the prospect of legal challenges in holding the medical professionals responsible for their oversights and possible failure to treat her husband effectively. Lois was full of intellectual questions and searching. Spiritually, Lois was angry that in spite of her fervent prayers, God allowed her husband to die, in what she saw as a senseless way. In other cases where the cause of death was an accident, a failure to perceive or receive proper care or death occurring from an undetermined or undefined cause, the anger felt by the bereaved can overshadow the other emotions making it especially challenging for the bereaved to progress in their navigation of the River of Grief.

Lois also felt some spiritual fear. Although she had met her husband at church, there was an acknowledgment that she didn't know the state of his relationship with God. His faith was not something he talked about and Lois felt some anxiety that he would be at peace, that his soul would find rest with the Lord. Lois' theological concept of salvation required that her husband surrender to the love and sanctifying power of God. Some of her spiritual anxiety was the result of her fear that her husband had not asked for forgiveness, nor accepted the Lord.

The challenge of the grief experience can also be exacerbated by previous grief experiences. In the case of Tabitha, the loss of her brother was exacerbated by the previous loss of her husband. Tabitha's husband suffered from lung cancer and was ill for seven years. The final four months were the most difficult for him and for her. Nearly two years later her brother, who had been ill with depression and subsequent substance abuse, died as the result of heart disease complicated by diabetes. The brother had moved to Arizona to be near his son and Tabitha felt the loss of both his moving away and his death very deeply. She regretted not being able to be physically present with him; a visit had been planned but he died before she could see him.

Tabitha and her brother were very close and she felt the loss as if it were a deep cavern in her heart and life. He brother's death brought back many of the same feelings of loss she had when she had navigated the River of Grief after the loss of her husband. It was as if this new River of Grief was simply a tributary of the original River of Grief, a tributary that brought her back full-circle to the original River of Grief she entered when her husband died.

Tabitha articulated the strain of having to plan a second funeral, a memorial service, so soon after planning her husband's service. She hadn't realized the anxiety that planning the second service would unearth. Tabitha had expected her brother's children to be a part of the planning, but that was not the case. They left the decision making to Tabitha and in one case, didn't even travel north for the service. Tabitha expressed the deep-seated anger the children had for their father. She felt burdened by their expectations and her own sense of responsibility to care for her brother.

Tabitha related that she had tried to find avenues to express her own anger, when she lost her husband and again when she lost her brother, so she would not continue to be burdened by it. She wished that her brother's children had managed their own emotions and anger at the time of their parents' divorce. Tabitha expressed regret that her niece and nephew, who were not present at the memorial service, did not have an opportunity to learn more about their father and his relationships with others by speaking with people at the memorial service or the reception afterward. Tabitha felt she carried these stories of relationships for her family.

In my own family, my sister encountered some of the same responsibilities and frustrations. Although she and her husband had been divorced for three years, her ex-husband's family relied on her to coordinate his memorial service, cremation, and to arrange for his internment without their input or support. My sister, who has experienced myriad deaths, the loss of a teenage son to suicide as well as the loss of both our parents, was thought to be "the experienced one" who could handle all the details. My sister was burdened with her own grief and loss, the loss felt by her two daughters, then aged 17 and 21, and the lack of support from her ex-husband's family. This burdening on one family member generated a lot of anger and frustration that made the remainder of the River of Grief journey more difficult. She was left to tell the story of his life and be the keeper of their mutual history, for her daughters', and perhaps even her own, sake.

As the result of the deaths in her family, Tabitha felt the responsibility to be the keeper of the family histories — both for her brother and their parents, and for her children. This sense of responsibility was felt anew as she began navigating the River of Grief following her brother's death. It reaffirmed for her the role she had with her own children and grandchildren as the keeper of family memories and history. There was regret in Tabitha's voice as she shared this sense of responsibility. There was no one to share this burden with. The burden was not just emotional, but was also physical. Tabitha was preparing the sell her home and was "weighed down" by the choices of moving memories as well as belongings. Even though there was an element of hope in her voice, her physical presence slumped as she spoke about letting go and moving on to a new setting, without some of the physical reminders of her family.

Moving on seemed to be a theme that helped individuals transition from the beginning of the navigation process to the challenging of the depths of the rivers of grief and then enabled them to move to feeling the flow of the river to a new destination. With each person I spoke to there was a need to put some things behind them and to prepare for what came next. "Bereaved people learn to 'let the past go' and turn their minds toward the future.[27] This involved facing the future, however bleak or dark or burdened the future might seem. Let us explore further the journeys of those whom I interviewed as we move into our discussion of the third stage of the River of Grief journey.

Stage Three – Challenging the Depths of the River of Grief

The third stage of navigating the River of Grief involves challenging the depths of the river. In this stage the bereaved works through grief as a struggle back from depression. Despair and depression can last a short time, for months, or even years. In some cases those experiencing depression felt frozen, unable to move forward in their navigation of the River of Grief. It was as if the river

27   Vaughn, F. Bruce. "Recovering Grief in the Age of Grief Recovery," *The Journal of Pastoral Theology.* Vol. 13. No. 1, June 2003, p 46

had become a dead and stagnate place and the life of the bereaved felt just as dead and stagnant. This might be equated to one who is sailing, relying on the movement of the wind to move, who stalls progress when the wind stalls. For anglers, quiet pools of water without movement may be where the fish are but for the bereaved feeling stuck and unable to move seemed endless. Challenging the depths and stagnant places in the River of Grief involves facing the future without the deceased.

In my own pastorates, I encountered bereaved individuals who seemed frozen in the depths of the River of Grief for many weeks or months. In other cases, there was sadness at the loss but no stagnation. The bereaved seemed able to face the future. Sunderland would describe this stage as the need to, "learn to let go of the past and turn their minds toward the future."[28] Letting go of the past was difficult for many people. The bereaved may feel that continuing to live is disloyal to the deceased; or means the deceased is forgotten. That is not usually the case. Rather this movement might be interpreted as needing to paddle harder on the River of Grief while carrying the sorrow of the loss. One moves, but one is burdened in the moving. The key to this step of the River of Grief journey is the movement.

When I visited Israel, I was told that the real difference between the Sea of Galilee and the Dead Sea is that while both receive water from the Jordan River, only the Sea of Galilee allows the water to flow through it. There is no outflow in the Dead Sea. That is why it dies. To use this as a metaphor for grieving might be helpful. Sorrow at the loss comes into the life of the bereaved, is expressed and then needs to flow out of the bereaved. Failing that out-flow, the bereaved gets stuck in depression and loss, dying to the future a little every day.

28 Sunderland, p.46

In some cases pausing to recognize that there are an increasing number of good moments mixed in with the bad moments, an increasing number of good days mixed in with the bad days may be extremely helpful here. The bad days might not ever go away, but there were increasingly more good days in between. Sharing this insight with the bereaved is important, as we acknowledgment that we don't "get over" losing a loved one. Rather we "get through" it.

Challenging the depths of the River of Grief

The third major step of working through grief is struggling back from depression. The depths of depression can cause the navigation of the River to stop or can cause the Rivers of Grief to stagnate, to cease to move forward through the current of time. Of those I interviewed, only Lois expressed indications of current depression. This may have been because hers was the most recent loss, only three months prior to our conversation. Her fears about her husband's salvation also affected her spiritual and emotional well-being. However, each of the bereaved I interviewed indicated a period of sadness and depression during their River of Grief navigations.

Lois mentioned that the best thing for her in coping with challenging the depths of the River of Grief was keeping busy. She mentioned doing yard work, cleaning out the sheds on the property, learning to take care of the gardens and chores around the house as important means for her to conquer the weight of sadness and depression. Lois also mentioned scheduling time to get out of the house and keeping her mind busy as a means of coping with the sadness.

For Candy the move from depression to acceptance was the result of establishing regular routines in the other roles of her life. While she had taken a major role in providing care for her mother, she had spent less time with her own family and less time focusing on work. After her mother's death, Candy was able to focus on her work as an elementary school teacher. The routine of working in the classroom helped her cope. The order of her days, the busy schedule of an elementary school teacher, and the tasks of being a working wife and mother all helped Candy have an external focus, to have little time to brood. In addition to the work Candy had to do, sharing the loss with her coworkers and friends, with others who had losses, helped her move through the emotional depression and loss. Not long after her mother's death, Candy was in a university book store, where her son went to school, and she found a little book "When God Winks"[29] which has remained a comfort to her.

Christine, Sophie's granddaughter, mentioned the routine of work as important for her coping with depression and sadness. Christine was the youngest of the bereaved I interviewed, 24 at the time of her loss. She mentioned the love and support she received via emails from friends, fellow counselors from a summer camp where she has worked for several years, and phone calls. Christine also mentioned the concern and care expressed by her friends, but she mentioned that for some of her friends there was little understanding about emotional loss. Being physically present with Christine was what these friends could provide. Their physical presence helped Christine feel less alone and more "normal" doing regular activities with young people her age. In some other cases some of her friends thought she was hanging out with them too soon. Christine shared that she needed

29 Rushnell, Squire. *When God Winks: How the Power of Coincidence Guides Your Life.* (New York: Atria Books, 2002).

the normalcy of everyday interactions, doing the things other young people her age were doing as a way of coping with the grief experience. Christine also mentioned the need for a work routine, but recognized that even when she was trying to offer her best work, she was often more irritable with her students than she would have liked. She recognized this as a transition time for her, a time of moving through the grief (what I call navigating the River of Grief and challenging the depths of the river) into a calmer, less burdened state of mind and being.

Other supports, Candy cited, for moving out of the challenge of the depths of the River of Grief, included cards and calls from friends and colleagues, neighbors offering hugs and kind messages, and attending church. These supports were cited by others as well. Tabitha identified the presence of others, even those she did not know well, who brought food, shared memories, offered hugs, and sent personal notes, all of which helped her move through the sadness and depression. Sandy shared that her close friends were especially important for her movement through the depths of grief. She cited her best friend who understood best how to comfort her, who phoned often, held confidences, and was simply present for her.

Bob cited that his family and their presence helped him move through the depths. Bob's son stayed with him for a couple of months after the loss. This kept the house from feeling so empty without Sophie there. Bob specifically mentioned hugs, having people wrap their arms around him as a way to make contact with him and to ease the feelings of loss and the depths of depression. Liza also cited the support of friends and even strangers bringing food to the hospital, to the house, and following the loss. As a contrast, Sandy thought the bringing of food was not particularly helpful, with the exception of the reception following the memorial service. She wanted the care of others, but the tangible gifts of food seemed less important than the visits from her Mom's group of friends, who shared memories of and stories about her mother with her.

In every case, the ability to move through the challenging depths of grief included support from the pastor and the church congregation. The pastor's presence, often during the illness as well as the death, and following the death, was cited by each bereaved individual as a needed support. Even Micah the serving pastor, expressed the value of having a concerned pastor as a part of the support team for the bereaved.

In his case, the pastoral role was fulfilled by pastoral colleagues, rather than his mother's pastor. Micah also cited some of his congregation's membership as being pastoral in their support and nurture. In many cases, the pastor was the person who helped the bereaved "tell the story" of the life of the deceased. This pastoral role seemed particularly important to each of the bereaved with whom I spoke. During the time when the bereaved was entering the River of Grief, when they were beginning to navigate the River of Grief, and especially when the bereaved was challenging the depths of the River of Grief, the pastor had an important role to play.

In each case the bereaved I interviewed mentioned the pastor's presence as being important. The physical presence of the pastor was important, before, at and after the loss. The pastor's ministry of presence spoke of care and compassion, provided a sense of constancy, and in some cases, was expressed as an anchor which helped the bereaved not sink into depression caused by the loss of the physical presence of their loved one. The pastors were seen as connections with the church community, but more importantly as a connection with the spirituality of the moments, and as a physical connection with God through their presence. The care and closeness of the pastor was essential to Lois. She knew one of the co-pastors of her church very well, but began to see the pastor not just as a friend but as a spiritual support to her. Sandy remarked that her pastor was willing to hear her, to hear her needs, her fears, her concerns and to be with her as a co-journeyer on and in the River of Grief. Tabitha remarked that the frequency of the pastor's contact and his ability to share time and prayer with her was almost overwhelming. She had not expected or anticipated that level of time commitment, care or support, yet she saw the time, care, and nurture as essential to her navigating the River of Grief. For Candy, who had known her pastor for nearly fifteen years, some of her appreciation for the support of her pastor had to do with his knowing her, really knowing her and her life, before the loss of her mother. This prior relationship helped Candy open up to the pastor and enabled their relationship to deepen.

This reliance on the current relationship with the pastor was mentioned by Micah as well. The relationship with the pastor and with the church before the loss helped bereaved individuals know where their support was coming from, who would be available to them when they needed support. No matter how expected a loss was, there was an element of shock and knowing the pastor and the church community ahead of time, having cultivated a relationship ahead of time, helped the bereaved and the pastor journey together during the grief time. Cultivating the relationship with congregants ahead of time allowed pastors to assist the bereaved when they reached this point of their grief journey and needed to challenge the depths of the River of Grief.

In every case, the importance of the ministry of presence was accented. Pastors needed to be present with those who anticipated or experienced loss. From my own experience as a pastor, more congregants and family members mention my ministry of presence, my being with them in the hospital, at their homes, at the funeral home and my follow-up with them than almost anything else. However, I know and each pastor knows, there is limited time to spend with individuals. Yet, priority needs to be given to being present whenever possible.

Congregational support teams, friends, and family provide additional ministry of presence opportunities. Several of the bereaved I interviewed mentioned that one individual in the congregation coordinated the supports being given to the family at and after the time of loss. By coordinating the support for the bereaved, the bereaved were not bombarded with phone calls or visits and the support was seen as support rather than a burden. This was especially important after the memorial service or funeral, during the time when more distant acquaintances had gotten back to their own lives and had seemingly forgotten that the loss was still real and the grief was still challenging for the bereaved. Support seemed more available at the moment of loss, just prior to the memorial service or funeral, and just after the church services and receptions. It was in the days, weeks and months that followed the family and friends' departures and the conclusion of the formal service that contact, presence, and support was recognized as pivotal to the bereaved moving through and being able to challenge the depths of the River of Grief. Follow-up support, ongoing attention to the bereaved, and an intentional reaching out on the part of pastors and church members was cited as very important to the bereaved I interviewed. Hospice organizations were mentioned as having good models for support of the bereaved and linkages with hospice organizations can provide good resources for churches and pastors, even if the recently deceased was not served by a hospice[30] organization.

Several of the bereaved mentioned books provided to them by their church, pastor or a congregational support team member. The most often cited texts were those developed by the Stephen Ministry program, written by Reverend Kenneth C. Haugk, Ph.D. and are part of the *Journeying Through Grief Series*. The series was designed to be distributed at definite times during the bereaved's journey through the River of Grief. Book One, *A Time to Grieve* was designed to be sent or presented about three weeks after the loss. Book Two, *Experiencing Grief* was designed to be sent or presented about three months after the loss. Book Three, *Finding Hope and Healing* was designed to be sent or presented six months after the loss. Book Four, *Rebuilding and Remembering* was designed to be sent or presented eleven months after the loss. Additionally, there is a *Giver's Guide* which provided suggestions for the giving group or individual as well as sample letters that can be adapted to be sent with the books.[31] These and other resources are mentioned in Appendix

30 Hospice, accessed at http://www.hospicenet.org on September 26, 2010.

31 Haugk, Reverend Kenneth C. Stephen Ministries St. Louis accessed on line at http://www.stephenministries.org/griefresources/default.cfm/775 on September 15, 2010.

Two, which provides a list of resources and resource organizations for use in establishing a grief support follow-up program for the bereaved served and supported by pastors and church communities.

While resources shared are important to the bereaved, the attention, phone calls, and presence of the pastor or church members was the most important support cited by individuals challenging the depths of the River of Grief. At this stage of maneuvering through the River of Grief, the bereaved were struggling back to normalcy and through depression. Isolation made the transition from this stage of the journey more difficult and the bereaved that were more isolated became stuck and steeped in or stagnated in depression. Additionally, at this stage of the process, the bereaved I interviewed mentioned being taken by surprise by deep feelings of loss which cropped up or were experienced at unexpected times.

Christine mentioned being "blindsided" while viewing the movie "Up" with friends. ("Up" is called an animated comedy adventure about a 78-year-old man, who after the death of his wife, finally fulfills his, and her, life-long dream of a great adventure.) [32] In March, nearly six months into her grief journey, Christine went with friends to see what she thought would be a fun animated film. She said, "I was unprepared for how I would feel about the grief expressed in the film - the reminders of our own situation — I cried through the whole film. It was personalized for me but the crying was cathartic, it was important that I couldn't be detached." Her comments indicated that she thought she had gotten on with her life, that she had laid the grief to rest, but in reality Christine was still

32 Disney*Pixar, *Up*, 1995, synopsis accessed on line at http://disney. go.com/disneypictures/up/main.html#/epk/about on September 15, 2010.

immersed in the River of Grief. She was still journeying and the film touched a part of her that needed to express her feelings of loss.

Others whom I interviewed mentioned hearing a particular song, seeing a family picture, encountering something they would ordinarily have shared with their loved ones as moments when their grief resurfaced. In many cases, the individuals mentioned sharing this occurrence with their pastor or a close friend as a means of understanding what had happened and why they were reencountering feelings of grief. As already mentioned, Tabitha related reliving the loss of her husband when she experienced the loss of her brother. Micah related a similar reliving of loss when his mother died, six weeks after the loss of his nephew. He additionally mentioned that he relived the loss of his father at that time, although his father had died in 1977, 33 years before. Grief experiences seemed to be cumulative and unresolved feelings of loss sometimes anchored individuals in the depths of the River of Grief. Telling the stories of the deceased often helped release grief feelings, both from past losses and with the current loss of which the bereaved spoke.

This discussion brings us to the fourth stage of navigating the River of Grief, feeling the flow of the river to a new destination.

Stage Four – Feeling the Flow of the River of Grief to a New Destination

The fourth major stage in working through grief is to decide to take up one's life again, certainly a different life than before the loss, but a life with a past, a present, and a future. The bereaved at this stage begins to reengage with daily routine tasks, regular activities, and responsibilities. It is as if the River of Grief journey can be seen from a variety of perspectives — the beginning stage of entry, the secondary stage of beginning to navigate the river, the third stage of managing the shoals and stagnant places, and the point at which the bereaved exits the River of Grief.

As the bereaved works through anger, depression, and regret, clearly daily routine tasks have not been the focus. In some cases the focus has been surviving the day's journey on the river. The bereaved recognizes and understands the ability to focus on little else besides the journey and are willing to accept it. As the fourth stage is reached, a desire to return to the routine tasks and the regular responsibilities begins. The bereaved is still in excruciating pain, but he or she is ready to take the first step to a "normal" life.

There was no prescribed timetable for the reaching of this fourth stage of the River of Grief journey. As mentioned earlier, some of the bereaved moved back and forth through the various stages of the journey, sometimes progressing and sometimes regressing. Memories, feelings of loss, sorrow, and yearning for the loved one may continue for years. Memories, at this stage, begin to be of happier times spent with the deceased. Feelings of loss and sorrow continue but the bereaved begins to experience some happiness in their life, may gather with friends and laugh, and returns to "normalized" personal relationships.

Feeling the flow of the River of Grief to a new destination

For each of the River of Grief travelers I interviewed, there was a component of this stage of the journey. For some (Candy, Sandy, Tabitha, Christine, and Liza), returning to some routine tasks and daily work responsibilities helped in moving through the earlier stages of the river navigation. For others (Lois and Bob) the ability to manage the daily tasks came much harder. Lois learned to do some tasks simply to provide upkeep to the house, but there was no ease of pain in the accomplishing of the tasks. They didn't even seem distracting to her. She spent her time doing the tasks but dwelling on the sorrow of the loss; the tasks were not a comfort. Micah never stopped serving in a pastoral role, and he found comfort in addressing the spiritual needs of others and having the congregation and colleagues share their love and compassion with him.

Of those I interviewed, Micah, Candy, Tabitha, Christine, and Liza had most clearly moved into this stage of the River of Grief. Tabitha was in the process of downsizing to a smaller home, determining which of the things in the house, which served as bearers of memory and tradition, would be coming into her new future with her and which would be given to family members or sold. She saw her future in a different place, in a new way, separate from the home she had known, but connected to it in her role as keeper of the family story and history.

Micah continues his pastoral work but was contemplating other changes in his life — working less, possible retirement, and new roles in his personal and professional life. There wasn't a lot of sorrow in the letting go at this stage; the sorrow had been in the death of people he loves. Liza retired from her career as a teacher, but has filled her time with teaching Vacation Bible School, Sunday school, and participating in women's groups - quilting primarily — which feed her creative spirit. Her future was clear and as she stayed connected to her father, Bob, this connection was out of love, rather than out of duty, out of a desire to be with him, rather than a desire to replace her mother's role for him. Liza was talking about the plans for an upcoming family Thanksgiving celebration and about finding new ways to celebrate without her mother, but with her family.

Christine whose goal once was to be a famous artist, saw her future very differently since the death of her grandmother Sophie. Christine said she had seen the faith and love of her grandmother and it inspired her own faith and her own future. Art was still important, but connection with students, family, friends, and God was her new life goal. Candy was enjoying her work family and teaching at the elementary school where she works, but she was heartened by the time she now had to spend with her husband, her two grown sons, and her college-age daughter. She saw her relationship with her daughter as very important and recalled the unconditional love she felt from her mother and wanted to share that with her daughter. The legacy of Candy's mother continued and it helped define Candy's future.

All these individuals continue their link with the church and with their pastors. The pastoral role changed as the bereaved enter this stage of the River of Grief. Rather than co-journeyers on the river, the pastor at this stage became a coach, an advisor, who traveled along the shore within sight of the river traveler, ready to offer a hand, ready to share a word of encouragement of comfort, but not so intimately involved in the day to day journey. Written resources continued to be used. Those from the Stephen Ministry[33], as well as cards and notes of

33 Stephen Ministries St. Louis accessed on line at http://www.stephenministries.org/griefresources/default.cfm/775 on September 15, 2010.

encouragement were welcomed and useful in this stage of the River of Grief journey. Liturgically, participation in a Remembrance Service was very helpful. Additionally, linkages with grief support groups, managed by the church or other community organizations, continued to be useful. In the case of the death of a child, a group such as Compassionate Friends[34] could be helpful. The bereaved still wanted and needed contact with the congregation and the pastor, but a little more distance was acceptable at this stage. Remembering the anniversary of the loss was helpful and marking that occasion with a card, note, or phone call had been especially appreciated by the bereaved with whom I interacted. Bob mentioned his continuing to feel love of the congregation, receiving hugs and warm wishes from the congregation and the pastor as important. Contact cannot be lost. The most difficult thing for the bereaved individual was to have the congregation or the pastor "forget" the loss and be reluctant to mention the deceased. That felt like a betrayal and abandonment. The bereaved carried their loved ones with them, no matter how long ago the death was. Even though the mentioning the deceased caused tears and sadness to recur, ignoring the loss and the deceased seemed uncaring to the bereaved.

The journey of grief, navigating the River of Grief may come to an end, but the loss, the sadness, and the absence of the loved one was, and is, felt for as long as the bereaved lives. Care and concern included acknowledging this state of living with the absence, even into a new and different future.

Throughout the interviews held and the stories shared, it was evident that for these bereaved grief was and is a

---

34   The Compassionate Friends accessed on line at http://www.compassionatefriends.org/home.aspx on October 5, 20 10

journey. Their stories provided evidence for and definition of the River of Grief model as it has been defined. The River of Grief model is supported by the experiences the bereaved interviewed for this research. The journey these bereaved have made included the four components of the River of Grief model: an entry point, "Entering the River of Grief," navigation of varied emotions, "Navigating the River of Grief," movement through depression and struggling to let go of the past, "Challenging the Depths of the River of Grief," and beginning to shape a new life without the deceased loved one, "Feeling the Flow of the River of Grief to a New Destination." As we move from the research, we begin to explore the divine, theological, scriptural, and liturgical resources which are helpful during all stages of navigating the River of Grief.

Key to understanding the River of Grief model is an understanding about river switchbacks. During the navigation of the River of Grief, the bereaved may feel like they have just entered the journey. Realistically, they have encountered a switchback — not returning to their original entry point but able to see and feel the grief as intensely as when they began. Recognizing this irregularity, the movement almost to the beginning of the process is important to the bereaved and is one of the reasons I designed this model. Also, each time an individual encounters grief, they seem to reenter the grief process for all previous losses. This, too, is a characteristic of rivers, as the feeding tributaries feed into the larger river. Navigating the grief process requires, familial, relational, pastoral, congregational, and even theological support.

Chapter 3
Spiritual And Theological Insights In The River Of Grief Model

Research into the etiology and nature of grief began in the twentieth century. Freud was one of the first to research unresolved grief as one of the sources of unresolved depression. Freud even explored the work of mourning and pointed out that "reality testing" was important to the work of grieving. He came to believe that "in 'normal grief' 'respect for reality gains the day.'"[35] As other psychoanalysts continued this research, it became clear that grief research was "continuing only from the perspective of psychoanalytical theory."[36]

Erich Lindemann took the research a step further and began to explore the connections between acute grief and psychosomatic illness. He hypothesized that acute grief is a normal human response, but "bereavement, which he defined as a sudden cessation of social interaction,"[37] was more indicative of psychosomatic disorders. His research concluded:

1. Acute grief is a definite syndrome with psychological and somatic manifestations.
2. This syndrome may appear immediately after a crisis; it may be delayed, exaggerated, or apparently absent.

35 Ibid. p 22

36 Ibid. p 23

37 Lindemann, Erich "Symptomatology and Management of Acute Grief," *American Journal of Psychology* (September 1944), p. 141 as quoted in Sunderland, Ronald H. *Getting Through Grief: Caregiving by Congregations*. (Nashville: Abingdon Press, 1993)

3. In pace of the typical syndrome there may be distorted pictures, each of which represents one special aspect of the grief syndrome.
4. Through counseling, these distorted pictures can be successfully transformed into a normal grief reaction with resolution.[38]

Lindemann went further to determine that the duration of the grief experience is related to the effectiveness with which the individual did the grief work. The problem with doing the grief work was that the individuals tried to avoid the intense distress associated with grief and the emotional expression of the grief. This led to psychosomatic illness or actual illness in the research. The importance in the grief work was the acceptance of the reality of the grief and the recognition that memories needed to sustain the individual. Delaying the "normal" reactions to the loss led to more distorted reactions — "overactivity without a sense of loss, acquisition of symptoms of the last illness of the deceased, alterations, sometimes lasting, in the relationships with family or friends, exaggerated hostility, activities detrimental to the person's social or economic existence, or agitated depression."[39] Lindemann also was the first of the researchers to explore the concept of anticipatory grief — the facing of the imminent departure of a loved one.

While both Freud and Lindemann explored grief, their exploration was of grief as a psychological phenomenon, not as a spiritual journey. The reactions to the loss were of importance to them but there was no search for meaning, no recognition of the need for or value of faith and spiritual relationships in their research. Their focus

38 Ibid.

39 Sunderland, p 25

was on the mind, the psychological, rather than the spiritual. No spiritual basis, exploration of relationship with God or support of a congregational community was included in their research.

While I believe it is important to explore the psychological aspects of grief, I do not view grief as an illness, but rather as a natural human process, a reaction to loss. "Grief, the emotional response to a loss differs from the concept of bereavement or mourning, the "culturally patterned behavioral response to a death."[40]

Spiritual pain is as real as psychic or physical pain. The hospice movement has brought us some of the best research and anecdotal evidence of spiritual pain and its impact on physical and emotional healing. "Palliative care recognizes a complex relationship between physical pain (and other symptoms) and emotional and spiritual suffering. Physical pain itself can be exacerbated by non-physical causes such as fear, anxiety, grief, unresolved guilt, depression, and unmet spiritual needs."[41] Since these emotions can be manifest during the grief process, it is important to recognize that physical pain may be due to spiritual issues. Research completed by palliative care professionals indicates that "some spiritual suffering — especially in certain cultures — may manifest itself as physical pain or other physical maladies."[42]

Spiritual pain is described in NANDA (1994:49) as the "disruption in the principle which pervades a person's entire being and which integrates and transcends one's

40   http://nccc.georgetown.edu/body_mind_spirit/pain_distress.
     html accessed on December 17, 2014; (Andrews and Boyle 1995:
     366.)

41   http://www.endoflife.northwestern.edu/religion_spirituality/
     pain.cfm accessed on December 17, 2014

42   Ibid.

biological and psychosocial nature."[43] Spiritual pain and suffering may be caused by a loss of personhood or one's definition of their personhood; deep despair; and/or feelings of being abandoned by God.

Particularly in the case of anticipatory grief, grief experienced before death occurs, the knowledge that a person is dying may evoke anger, loss of hope and meaning, shame or guilt, and fear on the part of the person approaching death and those who are in intimate relationship with the person dying. Approaching death may provide an opportunity for spiritual growth, which is not dependent on previous spiritual formation.

Persons need not share a religious or philosophical framework that says that good can come out of difficult times or life out of death in order to experience growth and healing during the grieving process.

It is also important to recognize that spiritual growth does not diminish suffering. Yet, the permission to grieve and to withdraw from routine activities gives those experiencing grief time to engage in spiritual reflection and spiritual practices, to seek participation in religious traditions as a source of meaning, strength and comfort; to take spiritual risks one might ordinarily avoid; and to consider issues such as forgiveness, reconciliation, the afterlife and the value of life itself that are not usually considered. [44] Yet, not all those who are grieving are comforted by their spiritual beliefs.

"Anandarajah and Hight (2001) note that "spiritual distress and spiritual crisis" occur when a person is "unable to find sources of meaning, hope, love, peace,

43   http://nccc.georgetown.edu/body_mind_spirit/pain_distress.html accessed on December 17, 2014

44   http://www.endoflife.northwestern.edu/religion_spirituality/pain.cfm accessed on December 17, 2014

comfort, strength, and connection in life or when conflict occurs between their beliefs and what is happening in their life." Sources list multiple defining characteristics of spiritual distress that may cause or indicate the presence of spiritual pain. Stoll (1989) and Pehler (1997) list similar defining characteristics, although Pehler also includes characteristics from several other studies. For both, the major characteristic was an expression of concern with the meaning of life/death or any belief system.

The lists included, but were not limited to, anger toward God, questioning the meaning of suffering or the meaning of one's own existence, verbal comments regarding an inner conflict about beliefs or about one's relationship with a deity, an inability to participate in one's usual religious practices, and more."[45]

Annemarie Bezold, Coordinator of the Grief Program in Fairfax County Community Services Board in Virginia conducts a monthly support group for families who have lost a child either in pregnancy or in the first year of life. While some parents find strength, comfort, and solace in spirituality and religion as they mourn, others experience more of a "roller coaster" relationship with God. (Personal communication with author August 30, 2007). Some question, "How could a loving God let this happen?" Some struggle with their relationship with God as they go from angry, to alienated, and then for many, eventual comfort again when they reconnect with God.

Some find comfort by believing that their baby is in "God's hands" or has been united with deceased relatives. Some parents have viewed their child's end of life as a "spiritual journey." (Robinson et al. 2006). Not all parents find comfort in religion or spirituality when it comes

45   http://nccc.georgetown.edu/body_mind_spirit/pain_distress. html accessed on December 17, 2014

to grief as evidenced by Balzer (2003) who describes his unsuccessful efforts to connect with a god; but he was able to find a "more peaceful and accepting relationship with the world through the death of his four-month-old son."[46]

The focus of this writing has been on accompanying grief journey travelers from a spiritual perspective and using a spiritual approach. Accompaniment work requires energy, focus, compassion, care, and love on the part of pastors and congregations. Resources are available to assist the congregation and the pastor in co-journeying with those who are mourning. This chapter focuses on divine, spiritual, scriptural, theological, and liturgical assistance.

Divine Assistance

We will now explore encountering God as a means of divine assistance in the navigation of the River of Grief. Activities and practices of faith which bring us into closer relationship with God are explored.

The obvious resource for divine assistance on the River of Grief journey is God. Yet, much of what had been written about grief and mourning was about stages and steps of grieving and the psychological behaviors inherent to the stages. Much that pastors and congregations used as resources for co-journeying with the grieving was about helping people move through stages and steps of grief. Little was included about encountering God on the journey. As individuals of faith, God is at the center of our life experience. This is no less true when we are grieving. Therefore, seeking to recognize the presence of the divine is an important aspect of accompanying individuals through grief and mourning.

46 Ibid.

As was indicated, the individuals I interviewed were at different points in their River of Grief journeys. Each had an experience of faith and of the divine. For each the manifestation of God's presence came at different points on the journey and in different ways. Almost all of those interviewed spoke of prayer and singing as being avenues for encountering God on the River of Grief journey. Many spoke of congregational participation as important to them. Other faith practices may also be beneficial to the grieving. The specific activities of our faith can help us to connect with the divine, as these activities helped those bereaved who were interviewed encounter and connect with the divine.

Allan Hugh Cole Jr. mentioned the activities of faith as one means for helping the grieving. He defined the activities of faith as things like church membership or participation, worship, Scripture reading, mission work, and service to others, as well as prayer.[47] Cole encouraged the grieving to reflect on their faith practices and how they might help the individual connect to God routinely. These gave the individual insight into how the activities or practices of faith might help them to encounter God during the grieving process. He also identified three things these practices might provide to the grieving:

1. Deeper connection to God and others
2. A regular encounter with the Christian story, including its promises.
3. Through faith practices drawing deeper into the Christian story and what it says about life, death, and hope.[48]

47   Cole, Allan Hugh, Jr. *Good Mourning: Getting Through Your Grief.* (Louisville: Westminster John Knox Press, 2008), p.73.

48   Ibid.

Within faith practice was an opportunity to seek out that which brought God and God's promises into the current reality of grief and mourning. Faith practices reinforced the relationship with God and the encounters with God in all times of life, which was especially helpful to those encountering the River of Grief.

Worship and the reading of scripture are mentioned as faith practices beneficial to encountering the divine. Both these practices assist individuals with connection to the Christian experience and the "story" of what it means to be a Christian. The "story" of Christianity includes God's transforming and redemptive work in all of creation as viewed through the lens of the life, death, and resurrection of Jesus the Christ, as well as the presence of the Holy Spirit, our advocate. God's nature and work in the world and in individuals is clarified in the "story" of our faith. An understanding of God, God's restorative power, God's creative energy in the world, God's grace and love for humankind affect how we encounter all aspects of our life. This is no less true when we are in mourning or navigating the River of Grief.

Both these faith practices, worship and the reading of scripture, affect the way we see the world in relation to God. In Cole's words, "Here we meet God. Here God meets us."[49] To those I interviewed, meeting God and knowing God's presence was important. Faith practices, especially worship and the reading of scripture have helped many of us, and perhaps especially those navigating the River of Grief, connect with God and with each other in the "story" of our faith. Participation in a church community was useful in navigating the River of Grief

49   Ibid. p. 77.

and while there was some discomfort expressed in encountering individuals we don't know well within the congregation, this was generally outweighed by the benefits of community, shared relationship with God, and the opportunities for support. The communal aspects of worship provide shared relationship with God, shared roles in the Christian "story" and companionship on the journey. Those who are currently navigating the River of Grief can find others who have journeyed Rivers of Grief previously, or who may be navigating those rivers now. The support of others encountering similar challenges was very helpful to River of Grief travelers in interviews.

Worship provides an opportunity to explore our faith "story" as we encounter human life experiences. Scripture enhances both our Christian worship and our understanding of God, our relationship with God and our faith "story." We move now to an exploration of scriptural assistance for the River of Grief traveler and the co-journeying pastor and congregation.

Scriptural Assistance

Let's explore scriptures which could be introduced to the River of Grief traveler by the pastor or the congregation. Some specific suggestions of both Hebrew and Christian scriptures are shared.

Throughout both the Hebrew and Christian Testaments there are passages of scripture which are helpful resources for the River of Grief journeyer. A concordance is useful to the pastor in citing scriptural passages which have meaning in addressing particular emotions or spiritual needs. Caution needs to be taken to clarify the context of the scripture passages. No one passage speaks directly to the current situation in its entirety.

The River of Grief Model provides for the tumultuous experiences of grief. Being thrown into grief is traumatic and requires much of the individual. Gaining footing while grieving is as difficult as gaining footing on the slippery rocks at a river's base. At every moment a step forward can result into a fall into the depths of the grief experience. Apparent progress in the experience does not mean that regression or a switchback may not arise.

Hebrew scriptures

There are scriptural resources which can inform this tumult and allow individuals to experience this pain and angst as a part of existence. Perhaps the most notable, and noted, reflection of injustice of pain and loss can be found in the Book of Job. Job is righteous, not deserving of punishment, and yet he loses almost everything — home, children, wealth, status, and health. Job's relationship with God becomes one of questioning and anger but never one of rejection. Throughout the entire text, Job never doubts the existence of God, merely questions why God is allowing these traumatic and horrifying things to happen to him.

In effect the book of Job is an allegory for our human experience. We can live without doubting the existence of God, but still rail against the unfairness, the pain, the suffering and the loss that is part of human existence. Those who are immersed in grief, also need permission to be angry about the human experience, to experience the anger, denial and bargaining that are reflected in the Kübler-Ross model. Anger can be particularly difficult to express and anger at God particularly difficult for those from some faith backgrounds. Permission to express anger is vitally important and using the book of Job to explore the anger of a faithful individual can be helpful.

The Psalms can also be helpful in managing the emotional aspects of grief. Psalms of lament and pain which nevertheless affirm God's presence can be especially meaningful. The entire book of Psalms states that death comes to everything, save God. All that is created can, does, and will perish. It is a part of the natural order, the human experience and existence. Humans, through the psalms, come to recognize and appreciate their temporary and temporal existence on the earth. Death ends earthly relationships, earthly pleasures, and earthly existence. The fear of humanity is that darkness overcomes them, that they are cast away from all they love, that they are separated from existence, that they are separated even from the love of God.

Yet, the psalms also remind us that God is present. God is still with the lost and the grieving, and that even death cannot overcome the power of God. God rescues us from the gates of death and loss. To be separate from God, to lose our relationship with God is death. To retain relationship with God is to ascend into God's embrace, to overcome the complex and dynamic power of death and move into a place of comfort and hope. Psalms often share this lament and praise, this fear and hope.[50]

Psalm 30 is a mix of lament and praise, wondering about why God seems not to be there is countered with the assurance that God is always present, always loving, always steadfast. Verse 2 cries out in lament and relief: "O Lord my God, I cried to you for help, and you have healed me." Verses 6-10 also reflect crisis and lament: "As

50 New Interpreter's Study Bible, NRSV, (Nashville: Abingdon Press, 2003), pp. 835-836

for me, I said in my prosperity, 'I shall never be moved.' By your favor, O Lord, you had established me as a strong mountain; you hid your face; I was dismayed. To you, O Lord, I cried, and to the Lord I made supplication: 'What profit is there in my death, if I go down to the pit? Will the dust praise you? Will it tell of your faithfulness? Hear, O Lord, and be gracious to me! O Lord, be my helper!'" All these verses proclaim the knowledge of the existence of God, a history of feeling God's presence in the psalmist's life and yet, a feeling that God is now hidden, far away, not paying attention to the pain and the crisis the psalmist is feeling. People of faith who experience grief experience these feelings. In the midst of their personal loss, there is a temporary experience of the absence of God. There are questions about why God would let the loss happen. There are pleas for help in the pain of the loss, a desire to feel God's comfort, God's graciousness and peace.

Yet, the psalmist reminds us that God's anger is but for a moment and God's favor is for a lifetime. There are proclamations and evidence about the faithfulness of God and the transitory nature of our grief, pain and loss. Verse 5b indicates that, "Weeping may linger for the night, but joy comes in the morning." The psalmist reminds us that there is reason to hope, just as the light of the dawn overcomes the darkness of night, so too the light of the faithfulness of God overcomes the darkness of our human fear, loss, grief, and pain. Verses 11 and 12 also reflect on the power of God's presence in a life filled with lament, pain, illness, and fear. "You have turned my mourning into dancing; you have taken off my sackcloth and clothed me with joy, so that my soul may praise you and not be silent. O Lord my God, I will give thanks to you forever." God's power, God's love, and God's presence can overcome darkness, pain, loss, hopelessness, and grief.

Other psalms may be useful in navigating the River of Grief. Psalms of lament are particularly helpful for they reflect the deep pain, loss, or grief of the author, as well as faithfulness and a request for God's intervention. Psalms of lament have been identified as Psalms 3-7, 10-14, 16-17, 22-23, 25-28, 31, 35-36, 38-39, 51-59, 61-64, 69, 71, 73, 86, 88, 102, 109, and 130.[51]

Paul Wayne Ferris Jr. adds the following psalms to the list: 42, 43, 74, 77, 79, 80, 83, 85, 89, 94, 137, and 142 as for him they contain invocation, lament, appeal, a protestation of innocence, and/or a vow of praise.[52] Dietrich Bonheoffer indicated that the book of Psalms is the prayer book of the Bible.[53] I have recommended and continue to recommend the psalms to my own congregation and to those individuals traveling the River of Grief. The response from those I co-journey with has been positive; the psalms speak to them while they are, or when they were, on their River of Grief journey.

Walter Brueggemann shared the insight that the Hebrew Bible accents human trust in God. Trust in God can be a support for those encountering loss and navigating the River of Grief. Trust can help eliminate fear and can become foundational for healing. Brueggemann accents some psalms as revealing trust. He mentioned, Psalm 11, 25-26, 28, 31-32, and 55-56.[54] Additionally, the following

51 Ibid. p. 80

52 Ferris, Paul Wayne Jr., *The Genre of Communal Lament in the Bible and the Ancient Near East*. (Atlanta: Scholars Press, 1984),p. 93.

53 Bonheoffer, Dietrich. *Life Together/Prayerbook of the Bible* in *Dietrich Bonhoeffer Works*, vol. 5 ed. Geffrey B. Kelly; translators Daniel W. Bloesch and James H. Burtness; general editor Wayne Whitson Floyd (1996, reprinted Minneapolis: Fortress Press, 2005) as quoted in Cole, *Good Mourning*, p. 80

54 Brueggemann, Walter. An Unsettling God: The Heart of the Hebrew Bible. (Minneapolis: Fortress Press, 2009), p. 75

psalms accented hope in God: Psalm 25, 39, 69, 71, 130, and 146.[55] These psalms also might be particularly helpful to those individuals encountering the challenges of the depths of the River of Grief as a means of instilling hope for God's intervention, presence, and steadfast love.

There are a variety of other Hebrew scriptures which may be useful to the River of Grief travelers as they encounter the emotions inherent in the grief and mourning processes. 1 Samuel 1:1-23 reflects a bargaining emotional context through the story of Hannah, who bargained with God that if she bore a son she would dedicate the child's life to God. Hannah's faith allowed her to move through the bargaining into an acceptance of the will of God.[56] Esther chapter 5 relates to the burden of fear that Esther felt and then moves to her perseverance and the subsequent salvation of Israel. Job 19, 1-8 and 25-26 speaks of Job's "anger, desolation, and frustration, and ... also speaks of his faith."[57] This can be instructive to those who are traveling the River of Grief and who cling to the "I don't deserve this," expression of anger and who need further insight in order to cling to their faith in the presence of God. Isaiah 43 speaks of God's steadfast presence. Jeremiah 31 speaks of God's everlasting love. One or more of these Hebrew scriptures may be helpful as they reflect the emotional and spiritual needs of the bereaved.

Christian scriptures

Christian scripture readings may also be useful to the River of Grief travelers. John 14:16-17 is a resource for assuring those who are grieving of the presence of God

55   Ibid., p. 85

56   Williams, Donna Reilly & Sturzl, JoAnn. Grief Ministry: Helping Others Mourn. (San Jose: Resource Publications, 1990)., p. 51

57   Ibid., p. 71.

through Jesus and the Holy Spirit. Matthew 28:20 is another reminder that Jesus promised not to leave the disciples, the followers. Matthew 7:7-8, which encouraged the faithful to ask for what they need, is a reminder to seek God and ask for the hope and strength needed to navigate the River of Grief. Galatians 6 reminds us to bear each other's burdens, to seek to fulfill the law of Christ in this way. This passage can be especially meaningful to families who are grieving, reminding them to bear with one another as they individually, and collectively, journey the rivers of grief.

James 5:13-16 reminds the River of Grief journeyers to pray and that God responds to prayer. 1 Thessalonians 5 reminds us to pray without ceasing. Luke 11 and Matthew 6 both include the Lord's Prayer and can encourage River of Grief journeyers to seek God's attention through this familiar prayer. Any of the passages of the Christian scriptures which remind individuals to not be afraid can be helpful.

Scriptural parallels using water motifs

Water parallels in scripture are prevalent. Water is seen as chaos, is seen as having power over death and life, and is seen as having cleansing and healing power. Thus, a water motif is especially meaningful in relation to grief. As an individual enters the River of Grief, life seems completely filled with chaos. There seems a complete loss of control, no way to maneuver, fear overwhelms, pain encompasses everything, and darkness swirls in the heart and mind. The body may seem bruised and achy, in pain that has no apparent physical source. The monsters of fear, of anger, and of despair seem to be everywhere. Entering the River of Grief is painful, disconcerting, physically, emotionally, psychically, and spiritually overwhelming. The world seems unfamiliar and foreign, filled with tasks and ideas that don't mesh with regular human routine. All is chaos. Even though there may be people around to help, the grieving feel alone and isolated. No one can feel what they are feeling; no one can know what they fear or understand their loss.

From the first verses of Genesis through the Psalms into the prophets and including the epistles and the gospels, scripture is full of citations referring to chaos. Genesis 1:1-2 says, "In the beginning God created the heavens and the earth. The earth was formless and void, and darkness was over the surface of the deep, and the Spirit of God was moving over the surface of the waters." We are reminded that God alone can conquer chaos, can overcome it. "And they will pass through the sea of distress and he will strike the waves in the sea, So that all the depths of the Nile will dry up; and the pride of Assyria will be brought down and the scepter of Egypt will depart," (Zechariah 10:11).

Isaiah 17:12-13 says, "Alas, the uproar of many peoples who roar like the roaring of the seas, and the rumbling of nations who rush on like the rumbling of mighty waters! The nations rumble on like the rumbling of many waters, but he will rebuke them and they will flee far away, and be chased like chaff in the mountains before the wind, or like whirling dust before a gale." And the gospel of Luke shares the power of Jesus in 8:22-25: "Now on one of those days Jesus and his disciples got into a boat, and he said to them, "Let us go over to the other side of the lake." So they launched out. But as they were sailing along he fell asleep; and a fierce gale of wind descended on the lake, and they began to be swamped and to be in danger. They came to Jesus and woke him up, saying, "Master, master, we are perishing!" He got up and rebuked the wind and the surging waves, and they stopped, and it became calm." In all these cases, the human, created individuals have no control over the chaos, only God has control. Thus the grieving enter the River of Grief and know they have no control over the chaos of loss and pain. Seeking God in these first days may be the only way to regain any footing.

Water, seen as power over life and death, also well to the River of Grief model. Encountering death causes the grief-stricken to feel powerless. There is nothing we, as humans, can do to prevent death. We do a good job at prolonging life, but death comes to us all. When a death occurs, the grieving can feel drowned by the waves of emotions, like they are being tossed to and fro in the rapids of a river. The waves and rapids overtake them. There is no control over death or the changes in the life of the grieving. Truly the River of Grief seems in control. Individuals recall feeling overwhelmed, like their lives were completely beyond their control, ready to give up rather than try to regain their footing. Grief seems to have control over every aspect of life. There is nowhere to hide from it; nowhere to travel away from the overpowering sense of loss.

But water also brings life, natural and eternal life. In John 4:13-14, Jesus tells the Samaritan woman at the well: "Everyone who drinks of this water will be thirsty again, but those who drink of the water that I will give them will never be thirsty. The water that I will give will become in them a spring of water gushing up to eternal life." The question becomes, is the River of Grief life-giving? Certainly from the standpoint of eternal life, the deceased has been given access to eternal life — the cause of the grief is the movement into eternal life of the loved one. But is there life in the River of Grief for the grieving?

Isaiah 55:1 reminds us to come to the water: "everyone who thirsts, come to the waters." Is there life in allowing oneself to be carried into the water of the River of Grief? Is there relief in experiencing what is without trying to determine what will be? Those with whom I spoke talked about the need to feel what they were feeling, to be patient with themselves, to allow the feelings inherent in their grief experience to direct or lead the grief process. Much like the current of a river, the River of Grief allows the grieving to "ride along" to move with the current rather than to resist it; to use their energy to navigate and to feel rather than to direct the process.

Practicing one's faith at this point on the River of Grief journey can also assist the grieving. John 7:37-39 reminds the faithful Christian: "while Jesus was standing there, he cried out, "Let anyone who is thirsty come to me, and let the one who believes in me drink. As the scripture has said, "Out of the believer's heart shall flow rivers of living water."" Life comes out of the living, out of the experience, not from control of the experience. Jesus reminds the faithful to come to Him, to move into relationship with Him as life and challenge is experienced. Those with whom I spoke found comfort in the rituals and practice of their faith. Some recount the importance of faith community; some mentioned the importance of scripture and hymnody as part of the funeral or memorial service. Many found spiritual practices life giving and life renewing.

Water as purification and sanctification is also a biblical theme. If the River of Grief is seen as a method for uniting or reuniting with a faith community, with moving into a sanctified relationship, and/or as an opportunity to be cleansed of regret, pain, or anger, the grief experience becomes a purifying and sanctifying experience. Hebrews 10:22 reads, "let us approach with a true heart in full assurance of faith, with our hearts sprinkled clean from an evil conscience and our bodies washed with pure water." Letting go of regret for what was not said or what did not happen; releasing pain in a safe and blessed environment; expressing and releasing anger toward God, toward the deceased and toward medical personnel and caregivers, all these can be purifying and sanctifying experiences. The River of Grief, by pushing us along and allowing us to encounter these emotions, can move us toward reconciliation with the positive memories, the positive relationships, and the opportunities for remembrance as a health giving and life giving experience.

Theological assistance

We can now begin to explore theological assistance. A number of theologies will be introduced, including a theology of resurrection, soteriology or salvation, agapé love, and atonement. The River of Grief travelers may not perceive or understand that they have a theology of death but likely, especially in the case of those with some church attendance history, they do have some exposure to Christian theology. Even those with limited church or faith backgrounds, may have inherited some beliefs about death, the afterlife, conditional and unconditional love and/or punishment.

Theology of resurrection

If the River of Grief travelers have encountered the Good Friday worship remembering the sacrifice of Jesus at Golgotha and the subsequent Easter morning celebration of the resurrection, then they have had some exposure to Christian resurrection theology. Douglas John Hall shared his insights into the theology of resurrection and its decisive victory over death. "The resurrection of the Christ is decisive in this (Christian) Theology because it affirms that precisely in the encounter with ultimate nothingness God is ultimately victorious: Death cannot hold the source of life (1 Corinthians 15:55)"[58] An acceptance of a resurrection theology may comfort the grieving; leading to an acceptance that the deceased is in the embrace of God, rather than in the darkness of death and non-being. A theology of salvation may be comforting. As the bereaved reflect on their deceased loved one, their belief that the loved one is blessed by the grace of God and included in the family of God, saved through grace and welcomed into heaven, may be a comfort. Linked to this theology is a Christology which accents our redemption through Christ, our restoration to wholeness through the life, death, and resurrection of Christ.

Theology of soteriology

Soteriology, meaning the church's contemplation of the nature of salvation accomplished by Jesus[59] and therefore a theology of salvation, focuses on the restoration of our relationship with God, a restoration to our originally-designed wholeness and our need for restoration to that wholeness, and fulfills the doctrine of creation. We recall from Genesis that after human beings are created, it is written, "God saw everything that he had made, and

---

58   Hall, Douglas John. *Professing the Faith: Christian Theology in a North American Context* (Minneapolis: Fortress Press, 1993), p. 95

59   Ibid., p. 67

indeed, it was very good" (Genesis 1:31, NRSV). Restoration to wholeness through faith in God and God's grace, mercy, and redemption, a theology of salvation, moves us to be "oriented toward healing and fulfillment of humanity."[60]

Differences in the theology of soteriology need to be understood. Within the family, a wide range of theological values and beliefs may occur. The differences may not need to be reconciled, but the denigration or elevation of any one theory within the family may impact the completion of the River of Grief journey. Pastors may need to mediate across the differences in theology with the bereaved. A reminder that God's work through Christ is one of reconciliation may be useful in this regard. Additionally, reliance on scripture that places judgment of righteousness in the hands of God will also be helpful.

Theology of agapé love

An understanding of the theology of God's agapé love, which through Christ is extended to everyone, could be shared. When one enters into baptismal solidarity with Christ, one is raised into solidarity with God and with all.[61] The understanding that God through Christ accepts all of humanity is an important theological stance. Unconditional love is sometimes difficult for people to understand. We live in a world where so many relationships are conditional. Expressing God's unconditional and steadfast agapé love and exploring this theology may be very helpful to the bereaved. How have the River of Grief travelers encountered God's love? Do they believe

---

60   Ibid., p.272.

61   Hall, Douglas John. *Thinking the Faith: Christian Theology in a North American Context* (Minneapolis: Fortress Press, 1991) p.152

that God's love is shared freely with all human beings? Is God's love apparent to them in the support of their family, friends, pastor, or congregation?

As the research concluded, one clear finding was the need the bereaved had for love. The person interviewed expressed feeling the presence of God and God's love from pastors, friends, and church members. Bob mentioned the feeling of God's unconditional love expressed in the hugs of church members, Candy articulated the presence and love of God as found in her work group, as well as her church friends and family. Sandy felt God's love in the shared stories of her mother's friends. In each case, encounters with church members, family, friends, and pastors reflected God's love. Love did not answer all the questions. Struggling for answers while love was expressed was a comfort to the bereaved interviewed for this study.

Theology of atonement

Atonement and a theology of atonement also connect to salvation. The three theories about atonement are explored by Hall. These are the idea of deliverance or liberation, sacrifice on behalf of others, or revelation.[62] Each is present in the testimony of the cross and resurrection. How the River of Grief traveler connects atonement and salvation theologies together may impact their view of the future of their deceased loved one. Do they view atonement as a gift of Christ which liberates us from sin? Do they view atonement as the need to do something as an act of repentance? Do they see atonement as a revelation and recognition of the sacrifice made by Christ for our

62   Hall, Douglas John. *Professing the Faith: Christian Theology in a North American Context,* p. 403

salvation? Which view or which combination of views do they hold when thinking about their deceased loved one? As the River of Grief travelers reveal their thoughts and fears about the afterlife of their deceased loved one, the pastor has an opportunity to clarify, educate, and comfort the bereaved.

The other aspect of the theology of atonement which may need to be taken into consideration by the pastor is expressed by guilt or regret that additional actions on the part of the River of Grief traveler were not taken. Perhaps the bereaved was not able to be with the loved one when they were dying as was the case with Micah and Candy; perhaps there was a concern about an unresolved conflict with the deceased. Any regret or guilt may need to be managed with the pastor's assistance.

Theological conflicts

It is important to note that theologies of resurrection, soteriology, agapé love, and atonement may cause conflicts for the River of Grief traveler. As in the case of Lois, who feared her husband's relationship with God was distant and questioned whether he would be welcomed into heaven, reassurance based on God's grace, freely given and unearned, may be needed.

Pastoral support in interpreting God's grace, our justification through faith, and an understanding of God's mercy and steadfast love for God's created human family can impact the bereaved. The pastor needs to speak honestly and with integrity about their own and their denominational theologies, but this is not a time for abstraction. These are real questions and concerns being asked by real people who are in spiritual, emotional, intellectual, and in some cases, physical pain. Pastors are advised to act first with love and then with theology.

The questions for the pastor and the congregation become:

1. What is our personal and doctrinal theology about grace, atonement, salvation, and redemption?
2. Can we articulate what we believe about God's grace, atonement, salvation, and redemption?
3. Are we able to share the concept of God's mercy and steadfast love?
4. How will we share these concepts in a meaningful way with the River of Grief travelers?

Once again the theologies of resurrection, soteriology and salvation, agapé love, and atonement need to be articulated and rearticulated with the bereaved. God's mercy and steadfast love, along with God's understanding about our humanness may be important discussion points as the pastor and the bereaved speak together, before, during, and after the onset of loss.

Chapter 4
Liturgical Assistance
The Pastor And The Bereaved

Liturgical support for the bereaved gives the pastor a doorway into the grieving process of the congregation or community member. As individuals begin their River of Grief travels, liturgies can provide opportunities for expressions of mourning, loss, disappointment, as well as hope, gratitude, and love.

Liturgical assistance

More than one type of liturgy may be beneficial to the River of Grief traveler. The most obvious of the liturgies is a funeral, memorial service, or celebration of life. What this liturgy is called may be based on the denomination in which the pastor serves and the bereaved participates, or it may have more to do with whether or not the physical body of the deceased is present at the service. Another common liturgy is the committal or internment service. These are routinely performed at the cemetery or mausoleum where the remains or cremains will be interred. However, there are additional liturgies to be considered. Liturgies of lament, liturgies of spiritual healing, and remembrance liturgies are the most common additional liturgies. This section of Chapter Four will explore these liturgies and possible resources for use in the liturgies.

Funeral, memorial service or celebration of life assistance and resources

In times of grief, one of the most important methods of saying good-bye is the funeral, memorial service, or celebration of life. Each denomination has different outlines for these services, but some general facts and resources are helpful here, particularly for the newly authorized minister. First some definitions are in order. Funerals are generally worship services at which the coffin and body of the deceased are present. In some services the coffin is open until the close of the worship service, while in others the tradition is to process into the sanctuary with a closed and draped coffin. In any case, the presence of the body of the deceased connotes the worship as a funeral service. The placement of the coffin is generally at the chancel or near the front of the sanctuary where those attending can focus on it. The family often is seated in the first couple of pews or rows of the sanctuary or chapel space. Whether or not the coffin has been processed in or simply placed before the worship service, the coffin generally is recessed out of the worship space, with the clergy and family following behind.

In a memorial service, the deceased's body is not present. Cremation may have occurred and cremains may be in the sanctuary and/or pictures of the deceased may be provided. A memorial service may be held before or after the remains have been buried or may be held at a location where family is present but the deceased's remains are not available. With my own parents, two memorial services were held for each, one in North Carolina where they resided with my sister for a couple of years prior to their deaths and one in the church I was serving in northern New York closer to where they had lived the majority of their lives. The multiple services in multiple locations provided an opportunity for family and friends from all part of their lives to participate in the services. This may be an important consideration for the pastor and the bereaved.

Either a funeral or a memorial service can be called a celebration of life. Focusing on celebrating the life of the deceased individual provides an opportunity for stories to be told, for memories to be shared, and for the gifts, talents, and life of the deceased to be affirmed. The move from a more somber service to one which reflects grief but affirms the life of the deceased is fairly recent. The lament and grief is clearly an important part of any funeral or memorial worship service, but the affirmation of the life which has been lived is an important transition from past to future for the family and friends of the deceased. For most of those I interviewed, the celebration of life was an important component of their grief expression and the beginning of the navigation of the River of Grief.

Considerations for planning the liturgy

Planning a funeral, memorial, or celebration of life liturgy is a vitally important task of the pastor as the bereaved are navigating the River of Grief. Experienced pastors have, no doubt, developed their own practices, but with each of the bereaved I interviewed some important insights were gathered. To a person, all the bereaved I interviewed commented on the need for the liturgy to reflect the deceased person, their faith, and their family. I will outline steps that I believe are important in the planning of the liturgy.

First, no matter your denomination's format for the liturgy, a funeral, memorial service, or celebration of life worship service, remember the service is extremely personal and inherently challenging for the bereaved. Discussing the worship service is difficult. The bereaved want everything to be perfect, to reflect the love they have for the deceased, and yet, they don't know where to begin. Rather than beginning with putting pen to paper and filling in a template for the liturgy, pastor would do well to talk with the family about the deceased. Asking questions about the life of the deceased, the family relationships, favorite memories or challenges the family shared, as well as the family background regarding the growing up, school, employment or volunteer work, marriage, anniversaries of the deceased provide an opportunity for the family to begin to open up to the pastor and to each other. This is much simpler than determining scriptures and hymns at the beginning.

As the conversation flows from the family, encouraged by open-ended questions from the pastor, the pastor will get a sense of the family, the role faith and church has played in the family, and the readiness of the family to begin the actual planning of the liturgy. The pastor needs to come to this conversation prepared with a Bible, hymnals or a list of hymns, sample scripture readings, and some ideas to share with the bereaved family. These will be used a little later in the process but the family will be comforted by the preparation the pastor has made.

The second step is to ask the family how they would describe the deceased to a stranger. This description will give the pastor some cues into the important characteristics to accent in the liturgical planning and in the celebration of the liturgy. List these characteristics and then ask a further question, "What do you want me to be sure to share with people about your loved one?" Once again this may lead to more stories, but will give the pastor further cues into the characteristics of the deceased that will need to be accented in the celebration of the liturgy. Once this information has been gathered, the pastor may move on.

The third step is to ask the family if the deceased had a favorite hymn or a favorite scripture. Fairly often the family may not know the scripture reference, but they can identify a theme or a phrase. The pastor, who is not expected to be a concordance, can jot those phrases down and look up the passage later. While denominational guides may suggest particular scriptures, remember this liturgy is extremely personal and many different scripture readings can reflect the life, gifts, talents, and faith of the deceased. Hymns provide an opportunity to both determine the tone of the liturgy — is the family focusing on the resurrection, the loss, God's presence, God's grace, or an emotion such as love or compassion? Additionally, hymns give the pastor a hint into the theological views and approach of the family. Do they choose a hymn because it defines God or love or life or death for them? Particular hymns also have scriptural foundations and this can assist the pastor and the family in finding appropriate and meaningful scripture readings for the liturgy.

The fourth step is to find out if members of the family would like to read, sing, play an instrument, or speak at the service. A variety of poems, prayers, and scripture lessons lend themselves to family participation in the service. This is a time when a family member might want to share their talent in honor of the deceased. The number of speakers may need to be managed, but that can be done by informing the family members ahead of time about the total length of time the service should take. This is an important point to make. I once led a memorial service during which each of the four children wanted to share something about their father. Unfortunately I wasn't clear about the time constraints. The memorial service lasted two and one half hours, with each adult child speaking for between fifteen and twenty minutes. Needless to say, my lesson was learned.

As a fifth step, the pastor will need to gather additional information about graveside or internment services. Will one be held before or following the funeral, memorial, or celebration of life liturgy? Which cemetery is being used? Are there restrictions for burials at certain times of the year? For instance, in northern New York some cemeteries are closed once the ground is frozen or snow covered. If this is the case, a spring date may need to be set. In some rare occasions, the burial service is the only service being held. If that is the case, the previous four steps are important, but the liturgy will be much different than one celebrated in the church or even in the funeral home.

Finally, the pastor will need to ask any follow-up questions. Does the family plan to have a reception at the church following the service? If the church provides this, the pastor needs to share with the family any costs that they would be expected to cover. How many people do they anticipate attending the service and the reception following? Does the family want bulletins for the service? Are there soloists sharing music and what assistance will they need?

The pastor will also need to share whatever other fees are required. Many churches have a fee schedule for funerals. Be sure to leave a copy with the family. If you are waiving an honorarium for the service, tell the family. Organists should receive remuneration and you may need to assist the family in determining the amount if there is no fee schedule. Fee schedules can seem cold or distant but many families have no idea how to support the church in this regard and the fee schedule can be extremely helpful.

The pastor may want to discuss with the family what time they should arrive at the church, where they should wait before the beginning of the ceremony, how flowers will be managed, where pictures will be placed for a memorial service, and other choreography. I do not use the word choreography lightly. The comfort of the family is often dependent on their knowing the details of when to arrive, where to wait, when to enter the sanctuary, when to leave and where the reception gathering is happening. With family members who have experience in the church where the liturgy is taking place there is less need for this explanation, but those from out of town, those who are not regular church attendees, or those unfamiliar with church at all are comforted by the details being made clear to them. The pastor's role is to comfort and to make comfortable those who are traveling the River of Grief.

The pastor will then begin to lay out the plan for the liturgy. Denominational resources, as well as other liturgical resources, will be helpful in this regard. The following sections review some of those resources.

A word should be shared here about the message, homily or sermon offered at the funeral, memorial service or celebration of life. While it is true that the pastor has a "captive audience" for this liturgy and while the temptation may be to cram a year's worth of the liturgical calendar and a lifetime's worth of theology into the message, this liturgy is about a specific person, their life, and the lives of those who are bereaved. In some denominations it is expected that the theology and the affirmation of faith are important parts of the liturgy, as is an altar call for those moved to make a commitment to Jesus Christ. However, in most other cases, a focus on the life of the deceased, their service to their family, church, workplace and community is much more important. Linkage to faith, resurrection, and hope for eternal life, God's love and place for the deceased is vital, but the personal aspects are much more important than theoretical, theological or educational messages. The family needs to hear the connection between the deceased and God and the recognition of the uniqueness of the deceased during the funeral, memorial or celebration of life liturgy. Pastors may want to save the theological treatise for another time.

We move on now to the sharing of resources.

Denominational resources

Most denominational groups have a specific book of worship or another resource that provides the format for the liturgy of a funeral, memorial service, or celebration of life. In the United Church of Christ, of which I am an ordained clergy, the Book of Worship provides resources for the *Service of Thanksgiving for One Who has Died*. In the United Methodist Church, the *United Methodist Book of Worship* includes several orders of worship for funerals.[63] The Presbyterian Church USA and the Cumberland Presbyterian Church utilize the *Book of Common Worship* of the Presbyterian Church (USA), which includes a funeral service with many variants[64] The Evangelical Lutheran Church (ELCA) utilizes *Lutheran Book of Worship* that

---

63   The United Methodist Book of Worship, (Nashville, TN: The United Methodist Publishing House, 1992) information from Polman, Bert. Reformed Worship, Review accessed on December 1, 2010 at http://www.reformedworship.org/magazine/article.cfm?article_id=653

64   Book of Common Worship of the Presbyterian Church (USA), (Louisville, KY: Westminster John Knox Press, 1993) information from Polman, Bert, Reformed Worship, Review accessed on December 1, 2010 at http://www.reformedworship.org/magazine/article.cfm?article_id=654

provides planning resources as well as prayers for hope and healing. In other denominations similar resources are available. However, I want to share some multi-denominational or ecumenical resources that pastors and congregations may find useful.

Worship resources: multi-denominational or ecumenical

Over the years, a vast number of poems, articles, books, and worship resources come across the desk of a pastor or worship leader. Some of those may have resources useful in planning funeral, memorial, or celebration of life services. Compilation resources can be helpful. *Reinventing Worship*[65] a compilation of various worship resources with contemporary phrasing may be useful. It includes prayers that provide time for personal reflection, invocations, and prayers of comfort, thanksgiving, and a relief from pain. Ruth Duck and Maren Tirabassi include a "Service of Thanksgiving for Christian Dying into Life" in their resource *Touch Holiness*[66]. This includes an order of the rite of the service as well as the prayers, suggested scripture readings and recommended worship songs. *Psalms of Lament*[67] by Ann Weems provides contemporary psalms of lament that she wrote after the death of her son. They are a poignant contemporary resource for expressing grief. A particularly good resource with a focus on the lives of women is *Women's Uncommon*

---

65 Berglund, Brad. Reinventing Worship: Prayers, Readings, Special Services, and More (Valley Forge, PA: Judson Press, 2006).

66 Touch Holiness: Resources for Worship, edited by Duck, Ruth C. & Tirabassi, Maren C. (Cleveland: Pilgrim Press, 1990).,pp 156-163.

67 Weems, Ann. Psalms of Lament. Louisville, KY: Westminster John Knox Press, 1995.

Prayers[68]. This anthology of prayers includes daily life and stages of life prayers which focus on aging, trouble, divorce, grief, death of a child, and a myriad of other life rites of passage.

Poetry by Mary Oliver, Robert Frost, Helen Steiner Rice, Kathy Galloway, Howard Thurman, and others can be very comforting when used during a funeral, memorial, or celebration of life worship service. An assortment of quotes from poems and other resources are included in the Appendix Two of this work.

Conclusion

No matter the theology of the family, pastor, or denomination, no matter the comfort or discomfort with scriptural resources, no matter the history of church attendance by the deceased or the bereaved, and whatever resources are used in the planning of the funeral, memorial or celebration of life liturgy, the pastor and the congregation play important roles in comforting the bereaved as they navigate the River of Grief. The bereaved I interviewed spoke often about the joy of a meaningful liturgy, even in the face of sorrow and loss. Without the personalization, the story of the deceased's life cannot be told, and as Micah put it, "A fill-in-the-blanks sermon and service is no comfort at all." The co-journeying of the congregation and the pastor with the bereaved along the River of Grief is deeply evident when personal and individual care is taken to meet the needs of the family and to celebrate the life of the deceased.

This section of the text has provided some insights into the divine, scriptural, theological, and liturgical re-

68 Women's Uncommon Prayers: Our Lives Revealed, Nurtured, Celebrated, edited by Geitz, Elizabeth Rankin, Burke, Marjorie A. & Smith, Ann (Harrisburg, A: Morehouse Publishing, 2000).

sources which are helpful for pastors as they co-journey with the bereaved on the River of Grief. As we end our exploration of the River of Grief and its navigation by the bereaved, the final chapter will outline the conclusions reached through the interviews with the bereaved.

Chapter 5
The Formation Of Grief Support Groups

Pastoral Care Grief Situations: A Plan For Grief Ministry

Throughout my pastorate and in conducting the interviews conducted for this research, it became clear that many grieving families do not experience the pastoral response and support they receive as adequate. Micah mentioned the lack of personal detail shared by his mother's pastor during the memorial service, as well as the lack of subsequent contact by him. A number of individuals for whom I have performed memorial services in the last five years have expressed surprise at my follow-up with them and related the need for and lack of this kind of follow-up after previous losses. In these cases, the contact the pastor and congregation had with the bereaved ended after the funeral or memorial service. This was particularly true when the pastor was called upon to perform a service for someone outside the church or with no connection to the church's congregation. In these cases, many families felt ignored and abandoned days after the funeral.

Questions need to be asked about the continued support needed by the bereaved and how that support should be given based on the individual needs of the bereaved, with specific consideration to race, age, and gender. Based on the number of losses and congregant or family member deaths in a yearly period, the need for pastoral care and the number of pastors affiliated with the church or congregation, it may be advantageous to develop a lay pastoral care program.

Grief support groups may be a part of the pastoral care plan, but should not be its only component. Not all churches are prepared to establish a grief ministry program. If a pastor or congregation has no Stephen Ministry or Called to Care program, a hospice training program on grief and bereavement support may be helpful before beginning the development of a congregation-wide program. Some cancer centers and counseling centers have clergy training events on end-of-life issues and may be helpful in preparing the church and the pastor to develop a program for grief ministry. If a church congregation sees one of its ministries as caring for the bereaved within their church or community, specific guidelines and preparation need to be undertaken prior to the formal establishment of a Grief Ministry program.

Establishing A Grief Ministry Program

The first step of any grief ministry program is receiving the support of the leadership of the church. This may require some pastoral guidance, explanation, and direction. Whatever the congregational judicatory body is should be consulted and provide approval. Those who were recently bereaved should be invited to participate in the planning of the grief-support ministry.

At a gathering of the recently bereaved, the attendees should be asked specific questions regarding the grief support they received, the grief support that would have been helpful, what aspects of the support given them was of the greatest help and what was least helpful, as well as what they would see as an effective grief ministry plan for the church. An assessment of the church's grief ministry can be completed following this gathering, identifying strengths as well as gaps in the support provided.

One of the necessary steps in the planning process is to be sure that adequate family information has been gathered — birthdays, wedding anniversaries, dates of the deaths of members, and the family relationships of the members. Several church management programs enable churches to collect and maintain this data easily. A few of these programs are identified in Appendix Three. Remembering these dates and using them as points of contact, nurture, and support for the bereaved is important. The first year on the River of Grief journey is particularly difficult for the bereaved. Those I interviewed indicated that an acknowledgment of the difficulty with special dates and holidays along with a phone call, note, or pastoral visit was important to their continued healing.

As lay members are recruited to be a part of a grief ministry team, special attention needs to be paid to their personal gifts and talents. As the team members are recruited, they must also be trained. Plans for their supervision need to be developed. The training program might include listening skills, a clear understanding of grief processes and stages, acknowledgment that some grief behaviors are extraordinary and how those individuals are to be referred to one of the clergy, knowledge of funeral, memorial service, and committal service planning, and an understanding of the need for continuing pastoral care for the bereaved. Specific training may be provided to help the team understand the impact of loss on children and adolescents. Special attention may need to be given to these individuals since most grief programs are for adults. Hospice organizations may be an excellent resource in this regard. The Compassionate Friends may also be helpful in supporting families when children have died.

As the grief ministry plan is developed, one needs to consider the length of time that a bereaved individual will be followed. In some cases twelve months is appropriate, but the pastor may need to be the one to make that determination. Each time a loss occurs in the congregation, a grief ministry team member needs to be assigned to the bereaved. They will need pertinent family data, including special dates, such as birthdays, anniversaries, and others significant days and dates for use in follow-up. A grief inventory instrument may be used to assist in the development of a specific plan for a specific bereaved individual. The grief care team should meet regularly with the pastor, dependent on the rate of losses incurred by the congregation.

The establishment of a grief support ministry can be one means for supporting the bereaved as they navigate the River of Grief. As mentioned previously in this work, a Called to Care group and/or the Stephen Ministry program can be good resources for the establishment of a grief support ministry. Without this foundational experience, it may be difficult for a church congregation to begin a grief ministry.

Appendix 1
Worship Resources

Denominational Resources

As mentioned in chapter five, there are a variety of denominational resources which can be used to plan funeral, memorial, celebration of life, healing, or remembrance services. A portion of the available denominational resources are listed below.

1. *The United Methodist Book of Worship*, (Nashville, TN: The United Methodist Publishing House, 1992)
2. *Book of Common Worship* of the Presbyterian Church (USA), (Louisville, KY: Westminster John Knox Press, 1993)
3. *Book of Worship*, United Church of Christ, (Cleveland, Ohio: The United Church of Christ, Local Church Ministries, Worship and Education Team, 2005).
4. *Book of Common Prayer*, (New York: The Episcopal Church, 1979)
5. *Lutheran Book of Worship*, (Minneapolis, MN: Augsburg Fortress Press, 2006)
6. *Book of Divine Worship*, (Mt. Pocono, PA: Newman House Press, 2003).
7. *The Covenant Book of Worship*, (Chicago: The Evangelical Covenant Church, 1999).
8. *Moravian Book of Worship*, (Bethlehem, PA: Moravian Church in America, 1995)

Non-Denominational or Ecumenical Resources

A variety of non-denominational and ecumenical resources were also mentioned in chapter five. Here is a more comprehensive list, with some annotations to assist pastors and congregations in planning a variety of worship services.

Funeral Planning Resources

- Berglund, Brad. *Reinventing Worship: Prayers, Readings, Special Services, and More* (Valley Forge, PA: Judson Press, 2006)

    This resource has a variety of contemporary prayers and readings divided by subject and by liturgical season. Included on the accompanying CD-ROM are litanies; prayers; resources for weddings, funerals, etc.

- Biddle, Perry. *A Funeral Manual* (Wm. B. Eerdsman Publishing Company, 1994)

    This resource provides pastors with guidelines for planning and conducting a variety of funeral resources. It also provides information for a church to develop a funeral policy in a local church and for educating a Christian community about death, dying, and Christian funeral services.

- Duck, Ruth C. & Tirabassi, Maren C. editors. *Touch Holiness: Resources for Worship* (Cleveland: Pilgrim Press, 1990)

    This resource encourages creativity and sensitivity, as well as theological integrity in worship. The work as a theme of justice and peace and is respectful of human differences in gender, race, and physical abilities.

- Duck, Ruth. *Bread for the Journey* (Cleveland, OH: Pilgrim Press, 1981).

    This book is a resource for contemporary worship services, including a funeral services. A variety of other worship resources are included in the text.

- Engle, Paul. *Baker's Funeral Handbook: A Resource for Pastors* (Baker, 1996).

  This is a comprehensive guide to conducting funerals which includes pre-planning resources and access to denominational services from nine denominations. It also includes special services for suicides, accidents, unbelievers, and children. A selection of quotations, illustrations, and last words can assist the pastor in writing spiritual messages for the funeral, memorial, and celebration of life services.

- Geitz, Elizabeth Rankin, Burke, Marjorie A. & Smith, Ann, editors. *Women's Uncommon Prayers: Our Lives Revealed, Nurtured, Celebrated* (Harrisburg, PA: Morehouse Publishing, 2000).

  This resource was written by clergy and lay women from all around the country. It is a compilation of prayers and poems and shares women's search for understanding life against a backdrop of faith. The resource contains a wide variety of themes and life transitions making it a useful resource for pastors.

- Long, Thomas. *Accompany Them with Singing: The Christian Funeral* (Louisville, KY: Westminster John Knox Press, 2009).

  This resource includes descriptions of how the Christian funeral developed historically, theologically, and liturgically. It also reveals recent cultural trends in funeral practices, including the rise in both cremations and memorial services. The resource includes the basic pattern for a funeral service, provides options in funeral planning, characterizes a "good funeral," and provides preaching guidance.

- Weems, Ann. *Psalms of Lament.* (Louisville, KY: Westminster John Knox Press, 1995.)

  This resource includes the raw emotion of the mourning individual. In Weems' poetic style, with a Hebrew Psalm format, Weems reveals the emotions of her grief to God. The emotions felt by Weems may be shared by the bereaved a pastor is encountering making this a useful liturgical resource.

- Malphurs, Aubrey & Willhite, Keith. *A Contemporary Handbook for Weddings & Funerals and Other Occasions.* (Grand Rapids, MI: Kregel Publications, 2003)

   This resource is packed both traditional and fresh approaches for a variety of services and ceremonies. It includes complete services, sample messages, wedding vows, help for difficult funerals and memorials and guidelines for other special occasions

Resources For Healing Services

- Epperly, Bruce G. *Healing Worship: Purpose and Practice* (Cleveland, OH: Pilgrim Press, 2006)

   This resource is designed to assist pastors and other church leaders to integrate healing services into the total life of the church. It focuses on using a holistic approach, connecting healing liturgies with the theology, pastoral care, and social concerns of the church. Practical tools for healing homilies and liturgies are provided as well as theological reflection on the healing ministry of the church, pastoral self-care, and congregational health care ministries.

- Juliuson, Eva. *Prayers for Healing* (Lima, OH: CSS Publishing, 2001).

   This book helps readers examine why we should pray for healing and how to do it effectively. It includes a healing service with prayers and Bible readings which can be used as a template for use in church services, a home, a hospital, or a nursing home.

- Oglesby, William. *Healing Touch: The Church's Forgotten Language* (Louisville, KY: Westminster John Knox Press, 1994).

  This resource educates clergy and laity in ways to re-claim the church's concept of healing touch. He provides models for determining when pastoral care might include touch, the laying on of hands, or when a referral for body-touch therapies might be made.

- Wagner, James. *Healing Services: Just in Time series* (Nash-ville: Abingdon Press, 2007).

Other Readings And Resources

A variety of other readings, poetry and prayers resources are available for the pastor. A partial list of some authors and works is provided here. A pastor may want to begin a file of quotes and poems which speak of life, a celebration of life, sorrow, grief, or saying good-bye as a means of increasing the available resources for use in funeral, memorial, and celebration of life services.

- Writings from Hildegard of Bingen, Karl Barth, Rainer Marie Rilke, Anthony Bloom, Garth House, Floyd Faust, M. J. Ryan, Joshua Loth Liebman, and Pierre Teilhard de Chardin.
- Poems by Ann McKenzie, T. S. Eliot, Mary Oliver, Jane Wilson Joyce, C. W. Leadbeater, Helen Steiner Rice, Kathy Galloway, Barbara Hills LesStrang, Richard Wehrman, and Julie O'Brien.
- Prayers by Brian Wren, Louis Evely, Virginia Rickeman, Howard Thurman, and Walter Brueggemann.

There are also some anthologies or additional books of quotations a pastor might find helpful. Two that I have used are *Praying Our Goodbyes* (Notre Dame, IN: Ave Maria Press, 1988) by Rupp, Joyce, and *Quotations for the Soul*

(Upper Saddle River, NJ: Prentiss Hall Press, 1997) compiled by Rosalee Maggio. Once again, pastors and laity may come across writings which will be useful. Often family members will have a favorite reading, poem, or song they want to be shared.

Appendix 2
Grief Support Group Resources

A pastor or congregation may want to engage in the formation and administration of a grief support group. A variety of resources are available for such efforts.

Resources for Grief: providing support and education to those who grieve, www. http://resourcesforgrief.com/griefSupportGroup.php

The Grief Support Group Manual includes:
- Outline for an eight-week Grief Support Group
- Suggested format for group sessions
- Guidelines and etiquette for group members
- Attractive and informative Grief Educational Handout for each group session*
- Sample forms, including a Press Release, Group Applicant Intake Form, and a Leader's Weekly Report Form
- Special Grief Educational Handout for handling the holidays
- CD with copies of the Educational Handouts and Sample Forms, for easy printing

Grief Watch, www.griefwatch.com
1. Grief Watch Newsletter – access to current and past newsletters and articles from Grief Watch.
2. Helpful Links – a list of some internet websites and pages that we think might be helpful to you in your personal journey.
3. Grief Facts – free printable information sheets covering a variety of topics including general bereavement, men and grief, death of a child, and more.

4. Articles – submissions from bereaved parents who have found comfort in sharing their personal experiences and from professional caregivers who have spent many years working with bereaved families.
5. Support Groups – a short list of support groups that may be available for you either in your local community or online.
6. Conferences – a link to information about upcoming conferences that Grief Watch may be attending.

GriefShare. www.griefshare.org

GriefShare groups meet weekly to help you face these challenges and move toward rebuilding your life. Each GriefShare session has three distinct elements: Video seminar with experts; Support group discussion with focus; Personal study and reflection

In addition to these resources, local Hospice Centers and Funeral Homes may host groups, provide resources, and have connections with whom congregations can find guidance.

Appendix 3
Learnings From The Research Study

Throughout the exploration of the grief experience of those interviewed, the analysis of the Rivers of Grief the bereaved navigate, the study of stages and steps of grief as analyzed by others, and the research into resources to support the bereaved, there was only one constant and that is the first learning. The first learning was that there is no one, consistent manner in which one grieves or through which one navigates the River of Grief. This finding may have been assumed before the onset of this study, but it is better to know through study and qualitative evaluation the individualized aspects of navigating the River of Grief.

Throughout the data gathered, there were some similarities in the needs expressed by the bereaved interviewed: contact with a pastoral co-journeyer, connection with family and friends, time and the opportunity to tell stories of the life of the deceased, especially in relationship to the bereaved, and the need for meaningful liturgy to celebrate the life of the deceased. Yet, each bereaved individual navigated the River of Grief in his or her own manner, at his or her own pace, and required different supports from pastors, congregations, support groups, and friends. The "cookie cutter" approach did not and does not work in helping the bereaved. In fact, the "cookie cutter" approach was the least helpful. Individuals needed individual care and consideration.

A second learning was that bereaved individuals may choose to reveal or hide how they progress in the navigation of the River of Grief. As noted through my interviews with the bereaved, some individuals were more forthcoming about their needs. Some individuals used the River of Grief navigation as a means to re-establish contact with family, friends, or a church community. Other individuals strengthened their relationships with the church community or pastor. Still others chose to distance themselves from the church. In my work with bereaved individuals, some found it very difficult to return to the church community because of memories of the deceased participating with them in worship or church activities. Their own participation then became painful after the loss. Pastors needed to monitor church participation and attendance, follow-up by phone and in person with the bereaved and monitor their physical, emotional and spiritual well-being throughout the time the bereaved were navigating the River of Grief.

A third learning was that stages and steps in navigating the River of Grief are neither consecutive nor chronological. Often the bereaved entered the River of Grief, began their navigation, and then moved back to the emotionalism of the entry point. Some bereaved moved through the step of challenging the depths of the River of Grief and then seem to move back to the beginning to navigate point. The pastor needed to become adept at discerning the point on the River of Grief the bereaved encountered at any moment and along the whole of the journey. Also, the pastor needed to insure that physical or psychological needs were being addressed. Referrals were an important part of this assessment. Not all pastors are skilled at counseling and psychological support and medical support needed to be provided by skilled and trained practitioners. Regular contact helped the pastor discern the progress the bereaved was making in navigating the River of Grief.

A fourth learning was that theological, scriptural, and liturgical resources are available to assist the pastor as he or she supports the bereaved. The pastor needed to explore the theological background and beliefs of the bereaved. Particular attention to the theologies of salvation, forgiveness, and resurrection were important to explore. In a similar manner, scripture readings were very helpful to the bereaved and a pastor should share particular scripture readings with the bereaved and specifically focus those scripture readings based on the stage of the River of Grief journey the bereaved was encountering. Denominational resources for liturgy development are certainly available, but other more contemporary, ecumenical and literary resources may also be helpful. A variety of liturgies were useful to the bereaved, from healing rituals prior to death to the remembrance service held annually or on the anniversary of a loss to an individual or a church community.

A fifth learning was that supporting the bereaved takes needs analysis and time. Pastors and congregations need to take the time to be supportive of the grieving, no matter how long the navigation of the River of Grief takes. Pastors present with individuals and their families prior to a death, have an advantage by being able to understand the family dynamics a little better than those pastors who were not present during the last stages of life. Pastors, who know the bereaved well, because the bereaved have been active in the church congregation, certainly have an advantage in being able to assess some of the bereaved's needs. In any case, some time for assessment of the needs the family has to be taken. Adding the assessment time, the liturgy planning time and the co-journeying time together, there is a large time investment in the care for the bereaved journeyers of the River of Grief. It may be helpful for pastors and congregations to develop pastoral grief ministries.

Conclusion

As I began to explore the topic of grief for this doctoral work, my own grief experiences were a great influence. In 2007 my brother was implicated in a state-trooper involved shooting while attempting "suicide by cop." (Suicide by cop is defined as committing suicide by drawing a weapon on a police officer in a manner which requires the police officer to shoot.) In the ensuing fifteen weeks, he was in the intensive care unit close to death. I prayed consistently and desperately for his life, in spite of the knowledge that his survival would bring legal challenges and likely imprisonment, for perhaps the remainder of his life. It seemed to me that there was no "best case" scenario. As I wandered this journey with him, I spent many hours on the road traveling from home to the hospital, a nearly two-hour one-way drive. I had an opportunity to reflect on other grief experiences: the loss of a sibling when I was twelve and he was five, the loss of twin sons at birth, the loss of grandparents, and of in-laws.

While driving to the hospital, early in my brother's hospitalization, I heard a Casting Crowns recording of a song titled, "Praise You in This Storm."[69] The song's lyrics spoke to me in many ways about how I was being accompanied by others so that I could still praise God, even in this darkened place, even in this storm. Although I am a pastor myself, I was comforted by the words of pastoral colleagues and congregation members in ways that reminded me to keep praising, even in the darkened days of challenge. As I navigated grief and loss, my heart

---

69 Casting Crowns, "Praise You In This Storm" *Lifesong* (Provident Music Distribution, 2005).

was heavy, but my spirit hungered for and clung to hope.

From this experience I began to wonder how other people might have been comforted, challenged, assisted, or hindered during their grief process or their sense of loss by the words of pastors, hymns, scripture, and worship. There are few human universals but birth and death are among them. "To live a human life is to experience loss and grief."[70] I began to view grief as a river to be navigated. There is the entry point, the loss, which pushes the individual into a river of emotions and challenges. As we progress down this river the course is rocky or calm, sometimes alternately, but the journey continues. We might choose to avoid or deny the river of loss and grief, but in that case the river is encountered in other ways, a flood of chaos and emotion at some other point in time, like a flooding river looking for the path of least resistance. From my personal experiences came this view, this model for looking at and supporting the bereaved as they navigated their own River of Grief.

It was my hope that this resource would be valued by pastors, congregation members, and grief ministry teams, that the insights contained herein would challenge us to be better co-journeyers with those who are traveling Rivers of Grief, and that newly authorized ministers, as well as those with extensive experience would find resources to help them as they nurture and support the bereaved with whom they have contact. My prayer is that as each of us enters our own River of Grief we will find caring, loving, hopeful, and spirit-filled co-journeyers to accompany us. May it be so.

---

70 Sauve, Stephanie, Brummitt, Mark, Spilman, Robert, conversation on April 8, 2010.

Sources Consulted

Berglund, Brad. *Reinventing Worship: Prayers, Readings, Special Services, and More.* Valley Forge, PA: Judson Press, 2006.

Bonheoffer, Dietrich. *Life Together/Prayerbook of the Bible* in *Dietrich Bonhoeffer Works*, vol. 5 ed. Geffrey B. Kelly; translators Daniel W. Bloesch and James H. Burtness; general editor Wayne Whitson Floyd. 1996, reprinted Minneapolis: Fortress Press, 2005.

Book of Common Worship of the Presbyterian Church (USA). Louisville, KY: Westminster John Knox Press, 1993.

Bowlby, John. *Attachment and Loss, Volume 3.* Hammondsworth: Penguin, 1969-1980.

Bridges, William. *Managing Transitions: Making the Most of Change.* Reading, MA: Addison-Wesley Publishing Company, 1991.

Brueggemann, Walter. *An Unsettling God: The Heart of the Hebrew Bible.* Minneapolis: Fortress Press, 2009.

Called to Care, http://www.calledtocare.com

Casting Crowns, "Praise You In This Storm" *Lifesong.* Provident Music Distribution, 2005.

Cole, Allan Hugh Jr., *Good Mourning: Getting Through Your Grief.* Louisville: Westminster John Knox Press, 2008.

The Compassionate Friends, http://www.compassionatefriends.org/home.aspx

Davidson, Glenn W. *Living With Dying.* Minneapolis: Augsburg Publishing House, 1975.

DeVaul, R and Zisook, S. "Unresolved Grief Clinical Considerations," *Postgraduate Medicine*, 1961, Volume 59.

Disney*Pixar, *Up*, 1995, synopsis, http://disney.go.com/disneypictures/up/main.html#/epk/about

Duck, Ruth C. and Tirabassi, Maren C. *Touch Holiness: Resources for Worship*. Cleveland, OH: The Pilgrim Press, 1990.

Ferris, Paul Wayne Jr. *The Genre of Communal Lament in the Bible and the Ancient Near East*. Atlanta: Scholars Press, 1984.

Hall, Douglas John. *Professing the Faith: Christian Theology in a North American Context*. Minneapolis: Fortress Press, 1993.

Hall, Douglas John. *Thinking the Faith: Christian Theology in a North American Context* Minneapolis: Fortress Press, 1991.

Harper Collins Bible Dictionary. Achtemmeier, Paul J. editor. New York: HarperSanFrancisco, 1996.

Haugk, Reverend Kenneth C. Stephen Ministries St. Louis, http://www.stephenministries.org/griefresources/default.cfm/775

Hospice, http://www.hospicenet.org

Kübler-Ross, Elisabeth. *Questions and Answers on Death and Dying*. New York: Macmillan, 1974.

Lindemann, Erich. "Symptomatology and Management of Acute Grief," *American Journal of Psychology*, September 1944.

Locke, Hubert G., *Searching for God in Godforsaken Times and Places*. Grand Rapids: William B. Eerdmanns Publishing Co., 2003.

McMahill, David R. *Completing the Circle: Reviewing Ministries in Congregations*. The Alban Institute, 2003.

Parkes, Colin Murray. *Bereavement: Studies in Grief in Adult Life*. New York: International Universities Press, 1972.

Rupp, Joyce. *Praying Our Goodbyes*. Notre Dame, IN: Ave Maria Press, 1988.

Rushnell, Squire. *When God Winks: How the Power of Coincidence Guides Your Life*. New York: Atria Books, 2002.

Stephen Ministry, http://www.stephenministries.org/stephenministry/default.cfm/917

Stone, HW. *Suicide and Grief*. Philadelphia: Fortress Press, 1972.

Sullender, R. Scott, "Three Theoretical Approaches to Grief," *The Journal of Pastoral Care*, December 1979.

Sunderland, Ronald H. *Getting Through Grief: Caregiving by Congregations*. Nashville: Abingdon Press, 1993.

Syreeni, Kari. "In Memory of Jesus: Grief Work in the Gospels," *Biblical Interpretation* Volume 12, Number 2.

The United Methodist Book of Worship. Nashville, TN: The United Methodist Publishing House, 1992.

Vaughn, F. Bruce. "Recovering Grief in the Age of Grief Recovery," *The Journal of Pastoral Theology*. Vol. 13. No. 1, June 2003.

Weems, Ann. *Psalms of Lament*. Louisville: Westminster John Knox Press, 1995.

Williams, Donna Reilly & Sturzl, JoAnn. *Grief Ministry: Helping Others Mourn*. San Jose: Resource Publications, 1990.

Women's Uncommon Prayers: Our Lives Revealed, Nurtured, Celebrated, edited by Geitz, Elizabeth Rankin, Burke, Marjorie A. & Smith, Ann. Harrisburg, PA: Morehouse Publishing, 2000.

CPSIA information can be obtained
at www.ICGtesting.com
Printed in the USA
BVHW042337120419
545421BV00008B/21/P